A Compila

CONTAINING THE

LECTURES ON FAITH

as delivered at the School of the Prophets
at Kirtland, Ohio
with added references on the Godhead and the Holy Ghost

---

also

AN HISTORICAL SKETCH OF THE SAME

by Dr. John A. Widtsoe

---

also a treatise on

TRUE FAITH

by Orson Pratt

---

also a

BIBLIOGRAPHY ON MELCHIZEDEK

by Ariel L. Crowley

N. B. LUNDWALL
COMPILER
BOOKCRAFT, INC.
Salt Lake City, Utah

TABLE OF CONTENTS

Historical Sketch of the Lectures on Faith 3

Lecture First 7

Lecture Second 13

Lecture Third 33

Lecture Fourth 41

Lecture Fifth 48

Added References on the Godhead and the Holy Ghost.... 53

Lecture Sixth 57

Lecture Seventh 61

True Faith, by Orson Pratt 70

Shem was Melchizedek 93

The Faith of Melchizedek 93

Bibliography from Melchizedek 94

Added Excerpts on the Godhead................40, 47, 53-56, 60, 69

HISTORICAL SKETCH OF THE LECTURES ON FAITH

By Dr. John A. Widtsoe

"In a revelation given December 27, 1832, the Lord commanded the establishment of a School of the Prophets for the instruction of the Saints. (See Section 88:127, 136-141; also 90:7.) The school was organized at Kirtland, Ohio, in February, 1833, and was continued until April. In this school the Elders of the Church "had many glorious seasons of refreshing and great joy and satisfaction beamed in the countenances of the School of the Prophets, and the Saints, on account of the things revealed and our progress of the knowledge of God." (History of the Church, Vol. I, pp. 322 and 334.)

"So well was the work done in the School at Independence that the Lord made especial mention of it, in one of the revelations given at about this time." (Read Section 97:3-6).

"The expulsion of the Saints from Missouri in the fall of 1833, and the consequent labors, appeared to prevent the continuation of the school in Kirtland during the winter of 1833-34. In November, 1834, however, preparations were made for the reopening of the school. The Prophet wrote:

" 'It now being the last of the month, and the Elders beginning to come in, it was necessary to make preparations for the school for the Elders, wherein they might be more perfectly instructed in the great things of God, during the coming winter. A building for a printing office was nearly finished, and the lower story of this building was set apart for that purpose, (the school,) when it was completed. So the Lord opened the way according to our faith and works, and blessed be His name,' " (History of the Church, Vol. 2, pp. 169-70).

"On December 1, 1834, the Prophet further said: 'Our school for the Elders was now well attended, and with the lectures on theology, which were regularly delivered, absorbed for the time being everything else of a temporal nature. The classes, being mostly Elders, gave the most studi-

ous attention to the all-important object of qualifying themselves as messengers of Jesus Christ, to be ready to do His
will in carrying glad tidings to all that would open their ears,
eyes and hearts.' " (History of the Church, Vol. 2, pp. 175-6).
    During February, 1835, the school was closed for the
season. . . .
    "It was during the season of the school of the Prophets,
held at Kirtland, Ohio, during the winter of 1834-35, that a
series of lectures on theology was prepared, which were
subsequently revised and printed in the Doctrine and Covenants, under the title, Lectures on Faith. The Prophet
makes this clear in his autobiography: 'During the month
of January, I was engaged in the school of the Elders, and
in preparing the lectures on theology for publication in the
Book of Doctrine and Covenants, which the committee appointed last September were now compiling.' (History of the
Church, Vol. 2, p. 180.) Evidence to the same effect is found
in the Messenger and Advocate, a monthly paper published
in Kirtland, Ohio. The reference reads as follows:
    " 'The following are two short lectures which were
delivered before a Theological class, in this place last winter.
These lectures are being compiled and arranged with other
documents of instruction and regulation for the Church,
entitled "Doctrine and Covenants of the Church of the Latter-day Saints," etc. It may be well, for the information of
churches abroad, to say, that this book will contain the
important revelations on doctrine and church government,
now extant, and will, we trust, give them a perfect understanding of the doctrine believed by this society. Such a
work has long been called for, and if we are prospered a
few weeks, soon shall have this volume ready for distribu-
tion. A full detail of its contents will be given hereafter.
    " 'In giving the following lectures we have thought
best to insert the catechism, that the reader may fully
understand the manner in which this science is taught. It
was found that by annexing a catechism to the lectures as
they were presented, the class made greater progress than
otherwise; and in consequence of the additional scripture
proofs, it was preserved in compiling.' " (Messenger and
Advocate, May, 1835, p. 122.)
    "The rank of the Lectures on Faith or their value in

comparison with the revelations found in the Doctrine and Covenants may be understood from the following statement taken from the authorized History of the Church: 'These lectures on faith here referred to, were afterwards prepared by the Prophet, and published in the Doctrine and Covenants under the title "Lectures on Faith." They are seven in number, and occupy the first seventy-five pages in the current editions of the Doctrine and Covenants. They are not to be regarded as of equal authority in matters of doctrine with the revelations of God in the Doctrine and Covenants, but as stated by Elder John Smith, who when the Book of Doctrine and Covenants was submitted to the several quorums of Priesthood for acceptance, (August 17, 1835) speaking in behalf of the Kirtland High Council, bore record 'that the revelations in said book were true, and that the lectures were judiciously written and compiled, and were profitable doctrine.' The distinction which Elder John Smith here makes should be observed as marking the difference between the Lectures on Faith and the revelations of God in the Doctrine and Covenants." (History of the Church, Vol. 2, p. 176, footnotes.)

"In the summer and autumn of 1833, a somewhat similar school was conducted at Independence, Jackson County, Missouri. Elder Parley P. Pratt who was the teacher, gives the following account of this school:

" 'In the latter part of summer and in the autumn, I devoted almost my entire time in ministering among the churches; holding meetings; visiting the sick; comforting the afflicted, and giving counsel. A school of Elders was also organized, over which I was called to preside. This also, to the number of about sixty, met for instruction once a week. The place of meeting was in the open air, under some tall trees in a retired place in the wilderness, where we prayed, preached and prophesied, and exercised ourselves in the gifts of the Holy Spirit. Here great blessings were poured out, and many great and marvelous things were manifested and taught. The Lord gave me great wisdom and enabled me to teach and edify the Elders, and comfort and encourage them in their preparations for the great work which lay before us. I was also much edified and strengthened. To attend this school I had to travel on foot, and sometimes with bare feet at that, about six miles. This I did once a week, besides visiting and preaching in five or six branches a week.' " (Autobiography of P. P. Pratt, pp. 99-100.)

(Note: The above is copied from the M. I. A. Manual for the year 1906-1907, Subject: Modern Revelation, pp. 32-34.)

The Lectures on Faith have not been printed in the current editions of the Doctrine and Covenants, because they are not revelations to the Church.

The preceding paragraphs will be instructive and enlightening to all, as it will give the information as to how and when these Lectures on Faith were brought forth, as well as their authenticity. The occasion for the printing of these Lectures on Faith at this time is because of a demand for the wonderful information that they contain. Surely, the printing of these Lectures will be the means of an increase of faith among all who read them.

LECTURES ON FAITH

LECTURE FIRST

On the Doctrine of the Church of Jesus Christ of Latter-day Saints, originally delivered before a Class of the Elders, in Kirtland, Ohio.

1. Faith being the first principle in revealed religion, and the foundation of all righteousness, necessarily claims the first place in a course of lectures which are designed to unfold to the understanding the doctrine of Jesus Christ.

2. In presenting the subject of faith, we shall observe the following order—

3. First, faith itself—what it is.

4. Secondly, the object on which it rests. And,

5. Thirdly, the effects which flow from it.

6. Agreeable to this order we have first to show what faith is.

7. The author of the epistle to the Hebrews, in the eleventh chapter of that epistle and first verse, gives the following definition of the word faith:

8. "Now faith is the substance (assurance) of things hoped for, the evidence of things not seen."

9. From this we learn that faith is the assurance which men have of the existence of things which they have not seen, and the principle of action in all intelligent beings.

10. If men were duly to consider themselves, and turn their thoughts and reflections to the operations of their own minds, they would readily discover that it is faith, and faith only, which is the moving cause of all action in them; that without it both mind and body would be in a state of inactivity, and all their exertions would cease, both physical and mental.

11. Were this class to go back and reflect upon the history of their lives, from the period of their first recollection, and ask themselves what principle excited them to action, or what gave them energy and activity in all their lawful avocations, callings, and pursuits, what would be the answer? Would it not be that it was the assurance which they had of the existence of things which they had not seen as yet? Was it not the hope which you had, in consequence of your belief in the existence of unseen

things, which stimulated you to action and exertion in order to obtain them? Are you not dependent on your faith, or belief, for the acquisition of all knowledge, wisdom, and intelligence? Would you exert yourselves to obtain wisdom and intelligence, unless you did believe that you could obtain them? Would you have ever sown, if you had not believed that you would reap? Would you have ever planted, if you had not believed that you would gather? Would you have ever asked, unless you had believed that you would receive? Would you have ever sought, unless you had believed that you would have found? Or, would you have ever knocked, unless you had believed that it would have been opened unto you? In a word, is there anything that you would have done, either physical or mental, if you had not previously believed? Are not all your exertions of every kind, dependent on your faith? Or, may we not ask, what have you, or what do you possess, which you have not obtained by reason of your faith? Your food, your raiment, your lodgings, are they not all by reason of your faith? Reflect, and ask yourselves if these things are not so. Turn your thoughts on your own minds, and see if faith is not the moving cause of all action in yourselves; and, if the moving cause in you, is it not in all other intelligent beings?

12. And as faith is the moving cause of all action in temporal concerns, so it is in spiritual; for the Saviour has said, and that truly, that "He that *believeth* and is bapized, shall be saved." Mark xvi. 16.

13. As we receive by faith all temporal blessings that we do receive, so we in like manner receive by faith all spiritual blessings that we do receive. But faith is not only the principle of action, but of power also, in all intelligent beings, whether in heaven or on earth. Thus says the author of the epistle to the Hebrews, xi. 3—

14. "Through faith we understand that the worlds were framed by the word of God; so that things which are seen were not made of things which do appear."

15. By this we understand that the principle of power which existed in the bosom of God, by which the worlds were framed, was faith; and that it is by reason of this principle of power existing in the Deity, that all created things exist; so that all things in heaven, on earth, or under the earth exist by reason of faith as it existed in HIM.

16. Had it not been for the principle of faith the worlds would never have been framed neither would man have been formed of the dust. It is the principle by which Jehovah works, and through which he exercises power over all temporal as well as eternal things. Take this principle or attribute—for it is an attribute—from the Deity, and he would cease to exist.

17. Who cannot see, that if God framed the worlds by faith, that it is by faith that he exercises power over them, and that faith is the principle of power? And if the principle of power, it must be so in man as well as in the Deity? This is the testimony of all the sacred writers, and the lesson which they have been endeavouring to teach to man.

18. The Saviour says (Matthew xvii. 19, 20), in explaining the reason why the disciples could not cast out the devil, that it was because of their unbelief—"For verily I say unto you" (said he), "if ye have faith as a grain of mustard seed, ye shall say unto this mountain, Remove hence to yonder place,' and it shall remove; and nothing shall be impossible unto you."

19. Moroni, while abridging and compiling the record of his fathers, has given us the following account of faith as the principle of power. He says, page 597, that it was the faith of Alma and Amulek which caused the walls of the prison to be rent, as recorded on the 278th page; it was the faith of Nephi and Lehi which caused a change to be wrought upon the hearts of the Lamanites, when they were immersed with the Holy Spirit and with fire, as seen on the 443rd page; and that it was by faith the mountain Zerin was removed when the brother of Jared spake in the name of the Lord. See also 599th page.

20. In addition to this we are told in Hebrews xi. 32, 33, 34, 35, that Gideon, Barak, Samson, Jephthah, David, Samuel, and the prophets, through faith subdued Kingdoms, wrought righteousness, obtained promises, stopped the mouths of lions, quenched the violence of fire, escaped the edge of the sword; out of weakness were made strong, waxed valiant in fight, turned to flight the armies of the aliens, and that women received their dead raised to life again, &c., &c.

21. Also Joshua, in the sight of all Israel, bade the sun and moon to stand still, and it was done. Joshua x: 12.

22. We here understand, that the sacred writers say that all these things were done by faith. It was by faith that the worlds were framed. God spake, chaos heard, and worlds came into

order by reason of the faith there was in HIM. So with man also; he spake by faith in the name of God, and the sun stood still, the moon obeyed, mountains removed, prisons fell, lions' mouths were closed, the human heart lost its enmity, fire its violence, armies their power, the sword its terror, and death its dominion; and all this by reason of the faith which was in him.

23. Had it not been for the faith which was in men, they might have spoken to the sun, the moon, the mountains, prisons, the human heart, fire, armies, the sword, or to death in vain!

24. Faith, then, is the first great governing principle which has power, dominion, and authority over all things; by it they exist, by it they are upheld, by it they are changed, or by it they remain, agreeable to the will of God. Without it there is no power, and with out power there could be no creation nor existence!

QUESTIONS AND ANSWERS ON THE FOREGOING PRINCIPLES

What is theology? It is that revealed science which treats of the being and attributes of God, his relations to us, the dispensations of his providence, his will with respect to our actions, and his purposes with respect to our end. Buck's Theological Dictionary, page 582.

What is the first principle in this revealed science? Faith. Lecture i. 1.

Why is faith the first principle in this revealed science? Because it is the foundation of all righteousness.
Hebrews xi. 6: "Without faith it is impossible to please God." 1 John iii. 7: "Little children, let no man deceive you; he that doeth righteousness, is righteous, even as he (God) is righteous." Lecture i. 1.

What arrangement should be followed in presenting the subject of faith? First, it should be shown what faith is. Lecture i. 3. Secondly, the object upon which it rests. Lecture i. 4. And, thirdly, the effects which flow from it. Lecture i. 5.

What is faith? It is the assurance of things hoped for, the evidence of things not seen (Hebrews xi. 1); that is, it is the assurance we have of the existence of unseen things. And being the assurance which we have of the existence of unseen things, must be the principle of action in all intelligent beings. Hebrews xi. 3: "Through faith we understand the worlds were framed by the word of God." Lecture i. 8, 9.

How do you prove that faith is the principle of action in all intelligent beings? First, by duly considering the operations of my own mind; and, secondly, by the direct declaration of Scripture. Hebrews xi. 7: "By faith Noah, being warned of things not seen as yet, moved with fear, prepared an ark to the saving of his house, by the which he condemned the world, and became heir of the righteousness which is by faith." Hebrews xi. 8: "By faith Abraham, when he was called to go into a place which he should afterwards receive for an inheritance, obeyed, and he went out not knowing whither he went." Hebrews xi. 9: "By faith he sojourned in the land of promise, as in a strange country, dwelling in tabernacles with Isaac and Jacob, the heirs with him of the same promise." Hebrews xi. 27: By faith Moses "forsook Egypt, not fearing the wrath of the king, for he endured as seeing him who is invisible." Lecture i. 10, 11.

Is not faith the principle of action in spiritual things as well as in temporal? It is.

How do you prove it? Hebrews xi. 6: "Without faith it is impossible to please God." Mark xvi. 16: "He that believeth and is baptized shall be saved." Romans iv. 16: "Therefore it is of faith that it might be by grace; to the end the promise might be sure to all the seed; not to that only which is of the law, but to that also which is of the faith of Abraham, who is the father of us all." Lecture i. 12, 13.

Is faith anything else beside the principle of action? It is.

What is it? It is the principle of power also. Lecture i. 13.

How do you prove it? First, it is the principle of power in the Deity as well as in man. Hebrews xi. 3: "Through faith we understand that the worlds were framed by the word of God, so that things which are seen were not made of things which do appear." Lecture i. 14, 15, 16. Secondly, it is the principle of power in man also. Book of Mormon, page 278. Alma and Amulek are delivered from prison. Ibid. page 443. Nephi and Lehi, with the Lamanites, are immersed with the Spirit. Ibid. page 599. The mountain Zerin, by the faith of the brother of Jared, is removed. Joshua x. 12: "Then spake Joshua to the Lord in the day when the Lord delivered up the Amorites before the children of Israel, and he said, in the sight of Israel, 'Sun, stand thou still upon Gibeon, and thou moon in the valley of Ajalon.' " Joshua x. 13: "And the sun stood still, and the moon stayed, until the people had avenged themselves of their enemies. Is not this written in the book of Jasher? So the sun stood still in the midst of heaven, and hasted not to go down about a whole day." Matthew xvii. 19: "Then came the disciples to Jesus apart, and said, 'Why could not we cast him out?' " Matthew xvii. 20: "And Jesus said unto them, Because of your unbelief; for verily I say unto you, if ye have faith as a grain of mustard seed, ye shall say unto this mountain, 'Remove hence to yonder place,' and it shall remove; and nothing shall be impossible unto you." Hebrews xi. 32 and the following verses: "And what shall I say more? for the time would fail me to tell of Gideon, and of Barak, and of Samson, and of Jephthah, of David also, and Samuel, and of the prophets, who through faith subdued kingdoms, wrought righteousness, obtained promises, stopped the mouths of lions, quenched the violence of fire, escaped the edge of the sword; out of weakness were made strong, waxed valiant in fight, turned to fight the armies of the aliens, Women received their dead raised to life again, and others were tortured, not accepting deliverance, that they might obtain a better resurrection." Lecture i 16, 17, 18, 19, 20, 21, 22.

How would you define faith in its most unlimited sense? It is the first great governing principle which has power, dominion, and authority over all things. Lecture i. 24.

How do you convey to the understanding more clearly that faith is the first great governing principle which has power, dominion, and authority over all things? By it they exist, by it they are upheld, by it they are changed, or by it they remain, agreeable to the will of God; and without it there is no power, and without power there could be no creation nor existence! Lecture i. 24.

LECTURE SECOND

1. Having shown in our previous lecture "faith itself—what it is," we shall proceed to show, secondly, the object on which it rests.

2. We here observe that God is the only supreme governor and independent being in whom all fullness and perfection dwell; who is omnipotent, omnipresent and omniscient; without beginning of days or end of life; and that in him every good gift and every good principle dwell; and that he is the Father of lights; in him the principle of faith dwells independently, and he is the object in whom the faith of all other rational and accountable beings center for life and salvation.

3. In order to present this part of the subject in a clear and conspicuous point of light, it is necessary to go back and show the evidences which mankind have had, and the foundation on which these evidences are, or were, based since the creation, to believe in the existence of a God.

4. We do not mean those evidences which are manifested by the works of creation which we daily behold with our natural eyes. We are sensible that, after a revelation of Jesus Christ, the works of creation, throughout their vast forms and varieties, clearly exhibit his eternal power and Godhead. Romans i. 20: "For the invisible things of him from the creation of the world are clearly seen, being understood by the things that are made, even his eternal power and Godhead;" but we mean those evidences by which the first thoughts were suggested to the minds of men that there was a God who created all things.

5. We shall now proceed to examine the situation of man at his first creation. Moses, the historian, has given us the following account of him in the first chapter of the book of Genesis, beginning with the 20th verse, and closing with the 30th. We copy from the new translation:

6. "And I, God, said unto mine Only Begotten, which was with me from the beginning, 'Let us make man in our image, after our likeness;' and it was so.

7. "And I, God, said, 'Let them have dominion over the fishes of the sea, and over the fowl of the air, and over the cattle, and over all the earth, and over every creeping thing that creepeth upon the earth.'

8. "And I, God, created man in mine own image, in the image of mine Only Begotten created I him; male and female created I them. And I, God, blessed them, and said unto them, 'Be fruitful, and multiply, and replenish the earth, and subdue it; and have dominion over the fish of the sea, and over the fowl of the air, and over every living thing that moveth upon the earth.'

9. "And I, God, said unto man, 'Behold, I have given you every herb bearing seed, which is upon the face of all the earth, and every tree in the which shall be the fruit of a tree yielding seed; to you it shall be for meat.' "

10. Again, Genesis ii. 15, 16, 17, 19, 20: "And I, the Lord God, took the man, and put him into the garden of Eden, to dress it and to keep it. And I, the Lord God, commanded the man saying, 'Of every tree of the garden thou mayest freely eat; but of the tree of the knowledge of good and evil thou shalt not eat of it; nevertheless thou mayest choose for thyself, for it is given unto thee; but remember that I forbid it, for in the day thou eatest thereof thou shalt surely die.'

11. "And out of the ground I, the Lord God, formed every beast of the field, and every fowl of the air, and commanded that they should come unto Adam, to see what he would call them. * * * And whatsoever Adam called every living creature, that should be the name thereof. And Adam gave names to all cattle, and to the fowl of the air, and to every beast of the field."

12. From the foregoing we learn man's situation at his first creation, the knowledge with which he was endowed, and the high and exalted station in which he was placed—lord or governor of all things on earth, and at the same time enjoying communion and intercourse with his Maker, without a vail to separate between. We shall next proceed to examine the account given of his fall, and of his being driven out of the garden of Eden, and from the presence of the Lord.

13. Moses proceeds—" And they" (Adam and Eve) "heard the voice of the Lord God, as they were walking in the garden, in the cool of the day; and Adam and his wife went to hide themselves from the presence of the Lord God amongst the trees of the garden. And I, the Lord God, called unto Adam, and said unto him, 'Where goest thou?' And he said, 'I heard thy voice in the garden, and I was afraid, because I beheld that I was naked, and I hid myself.'

14. "And I, the Lord God, said unto Adam, 'Who told thee thou wast naked? Hast thou eaten of the tree whereof I commanded thee that thou shouldst not eat? If so, thou shouldst surely die?' And the man said, 'The woman whom thou gavest me, and commandedst that she should remain with me, gave me of the fruit of the tree, and I did eat.'

15. "And I, the Lord God, said unto the woman, 'What is this thing which thou hast done?' And the woman said, 'The serpent beguiled me, and I did eat.'

16. And again, the Lord said unto the woman, " 'I will greatly multiply thy sorrow, and thy conception. In sorrow thou shalt bring forth children; and thy desire shall be to thy husband, and he shall rule over thee.

17. "And unto Adam, I, the Lord God, said, 'Because thou hast hearkened unto the voice of thy wife, and hast eaten of the fruit of the tree of which I commanded thee, saying, Thou shalt not eat of it! cursed shall be the ground for thy sake; in sorrow thou shalt eat of it all the days of thy life. Thorns also, and thistles shall it bring forth to thee, and thou shalt eat the herb of the field. By the sweat of thy face shalt thou eat bread, until thou shalt return unto the ground—for thou shalt surely die— for out of it wast thou taken: for dust thou wast, and unto dust shalt thou return.' " This was immediately followed by the fulfillment of what we previously said—Man was driven or sent out of Eden.

18. Two important items are shown from the former quotations. First, after man was created, he was not left without intelligence or understanding, to wander in darkness and spend an existence in ignorance and doubt (on the great and important point which effected his happiness) as to the real fact by whom he was created, or unto whom he was amenable for his conduct. God conversed with him face to face. In his presence he was permitted to stand, and from his own mouth he was permitted to receive instruction. He heard his voice, walked before him and gazed upon his glory, while intelligence burst upon his understanding, and enabled him to give names to the vast assemblage of his Maker's works.

19. Secondly, we have seen, that though man did transgress, his transgression did not deprive him of the previous knowledge with which he was endowed relative to the existence

and glory of his Creator; for no sooner did he hear his voice than he sought to hide himself from his presence.

20. Having shown, then, in the first instance, that God began to converse with man immediately after he "breathed into his nostrils the breath of life," and that he did not cease to manifest himself to him, even after his fall, we shall next proceed to show, that though he was cast out from the garden of Eden, his knowledge of the existence of God was not lost, neither did God cease to manifest his will unto him.

21. We next proceed to present the account of the direct revelation which man received after he was cast out of Eden, and further copy from the new translation—

22. After Adam had been driven out of the garden, he "began to till the earth, and to have dominion over all the beasts of the field, and to eat his bread by the sweat of his brow, as I the Lord had commanded him." And he called upon the name of the Lord, and so did Eve, his wife, also. "An they heard the voice of the Lord, from the way toward the garden of Eden, speaking unto them, and they saw him not, for they were shut out from his presence; and he gave unto them commandments that they should worship the Lord their God, and should offer the firstlings of their flocks for an offering unto the Lord. And Adam was obedient unto the commandments of the Lord.

23. "And after many days an angel of the Lord appeared unto Adam, saying, 'Why dost thou offer sacrifices unto the Lord?' And Adam said unto him, 'I know not; save the Lord commanded me.'

24. "And then the angel spake, saying 'This thing is a similitude of the sacrifice of the Only Begotten of the Father, who is full of grace and truth. And thou shalt do all that thou doest in the name of the Son, and thou shalt repent and call upon God in the name of the Son for evermore.' And in that day the Holy Ghost fell upon Adam, which beareth record of the Father and the Son."

25. This last quotation, or summary, shows this important fact, that though our first parents were driven out of the garden of Eden, and were even separated from the presence of God by a vail, they still retained a knowledge of his existence, and that sufficiently to move them to call upon him. And further, that no sooner was the plan of redemption revealed to man, and he

began to call upon God, than the Holy Spirit was given, bearing record of the Father and Son.

26. Moses also gives us an account, in the fourth of Genesis, of the transgression of Cain, and the righteousness of Abel, and of the revelations of God to them. He says, "In process of time, Cain brought of the fruit of the ground an offering unto the Lord. And Abel also brought of the firstlings of his flock, and of the fat thereof. And the Lord had respect unto Abel, and to his offering; but unto Cain and to his offering he had not respect. Now Satan knew this, and it pleased him. And Cain was very wroth, and his countenance fell. And the Lord said unto Cain, 'Why art thou wroth? Why is thy countenance fallen? If thou doest well, thou shalt be accepted. And if thou doest not well, sin lieth at the door, and Satan desireth to have thee; and except thou shalt hearken unto my commandments, I will deliver thee up, and it shall be unto thee according to his desire.'

27. "And Cain went into the field, and Cain talked with Abel, his brother. And it came to pass that while they were in the field, Cain rose up against Abel, his brother, and slew him. And Cain gloried in that, which he had done, saying, 'I am free; surely the flocks of my brother falleth unto my hands.'

28. "But the Lord said unto Cain, 'Where is Abel, thy brother?' And he said, 'I know not. Am I my brother's keeper?' And the Lord said, 'What hast thou done? the voice of thy brother's blood cries unto me from the ground. And now, thou shalt be cursed from the earth which hath opened her mouth to receive thy brother's blood from thy hand. When thou tillest the ground, it shall not henceforth yield unto thee her strength. A fugitive and a vagabond shalt thou be in the earth.'

29. "And Cain said unto the Lord, 'Satan tempted me because of my brother's flocks. And I was wroth also; for his offering thou didst accept and not mine; my punishment is greater than I can bear. Behold thou hast driven me out this day from the face of the Lord, and from thy face shall I be hid; and I shall be a fugitive and a vagabond in the earth; and it shall come to pass that he that findeth me will slay me because of mine iniquities, for these things are not hid from the Lord.' And the Lord said unto him, 'Whosoever slayeth thee, vengeance shall be taken on him sevenfold.' And I the Lord set a mark upon Cain, lest any finding him should kill him."

30. The object of the foregoing quotations is to show to this class the way by which mankind were first made acquainted with the existence of a God; that it was by a manifestation of God to man, and that God continued, after man's transgression, to manifest himself to him and to his posterity; and, notwithstanding they were separated from his immediate presence that they could not see his face, they continued to hear his voice,

31. Adam, thus being made acquainted with God, communicated the knowledge which he had unto his posterity; and it was through this means that the thought was first suggested to their minds that there was a God, which laid the foundation for the exercise of their faith, through which they could obtain a knowledge of his character and also of his glory.

32. Not only was there a manifestation made unto Adam of the existence of a God; but Moses informs us, as before quoted, that God condescended to talk with Cain after his great transgression in slaying his brother, and that Cain knew that it was the Lord that was talking with him, so that when he was driven out from the presence of his brethren, he carried with him the knowledge of the existence of a God; and, through this means, doubtless, his posterity became acquainted with the fact that such a Being existed.

33. From this we can see that the whole human family in the early age of their existence, in all their different branches, had this knowledge disseminated among them; so that the existence of God became an object of faith in the early age of the world. And the evidences which these men had of the existence of a God, was the testimony of their fathers in the first instance.

34. The reason why we have been thus particular on this part of our subject, is that this class may see by what means it was that God became an object of faith among men after the fall; and what it was that stirred up the faith of multitudes to feel after him—to search after a knowledge of his character, perfections and attributes, until they became extensively acquainted with him, and not only commune with him and behold his glory, but be partakers of his power and stand in his presence.

35. Let this class mark particularly, that the testimony which these men had of the existence of a God, was the testimony of man; for previous to the time that any of Adam's posterity had obtained a manifestation of God to themselves, Adam, their

common father, had testified unto them of the existence of God,
and of his eternal power and Godhead.

36. For instance, Abel, before he received the assurance
from heaven that his offerings were acceptable unto God, had
received the important information of his father that such a
Being did exist, who had created and who did uphold all things.
Neither can there be a doubt existing on the mind of any person,
that Adam was the first who did communicate the knowledge of
the existence of a God to his posterity; and that the whole faith
of the world, from that time down to the present, is in a certain
degree dependent on the knowledge first communicated to them
by their common progenitor; and it has been handed down to
the day and generation in which we live, as we shall show from
the face of the sacred records.

37. First, Adam was 130 years old when Seth was born.
Genesis v. 3. And the days of Adam, after he had begotten Seth,
were 800 years, making him 930 years old when he died. Genesis
v. 4, 5. Seth was 105 when Enos was born (verse 6); Enos was
90 when Cainan was born (verse 9); Cainan was 70 when Mahalaleel was born (verse 12); Mahalaleel was 65 when Jared was
born (verse 15); Jared was 162 when Enoch was born (verse
18); Enoch was 65 when Methuselah was born (verse 21);
Methuselah was 187 when Lamech was born (verse 25);
Lamech was 182 when Noah was born (verse 28).

38. From this account it appears that Lamech, the 9th
from Adam, and the father of Noah, was 56 years old when
Adam died; Methuselah, 243, Enoch, 308; Jared, 470; Mahalaleel, 535; Cainan, 605; Enos, 695; and Seth, 800.

39. So that Lamech the father of Noah, Methuselah, Enoch,
Jared, Mahalaleel, Cainan, Enos, Seth, and Adam, were all
living at the same time, and beyond all controversy, were all
preachers of righteousness.

40. Moses further informs us that Seth lived after he begat
Enos, 807 years, making him 912 years old at his death. Genesis
v. 7, 8. And Enos lived after he begat Cainan, 815 years, making
him 905 years old when he died (verses 10, 11). And Cainan
lived after he begat Mahalaleel, 840 years, making him 910 years
old at his death (verses 13, 14). And Mahalaleel lived after
he begat Jared, 830 years, making 895 years old when he died
(verses 16, 17). And Jared lived after he begat Enoch, 800
years, making him 962 years old at his death (verses 19, 20).

And Enoch walked with God after he begat Methuselah 300 years, making him 365 years old when he was translated (verses 22. 23).* And Methuselah lived after he begat Lamech, 782 years, making him 969 years old when he died (verses 26, 27). Lamech lived after he begat Noah, 595 years, making him 777 years old when he died (verses 30, 31).

41. Agreeable to this account, Adam died in the 930th year of the world; Enoch was translated in the 987th,* Seth died in the 1042nd; Enos in the 1140th; Cainan in the 1235th; Mahalaleel in the 1290th; Jared in the 1422nd; Lamech in the 1651st; and Methuselah in the 1656th, it being the same year in which the flood came.

42. So that Noah was 84 years old when Enos died, 176 when Cainan died, 234 when Mahalaleel died, 366 when Jared died, 595 when Lamech died, and 600 when Methuselah died.

43. We can see from this that Enos, Cainan, Mahalaleel, Jared, Methuselah, Lamech, and Noah, all lived on the earth at the same time; and that Enos, Cainan, Mahalaleel, Jared, Methuselah, and Lamech, were all acquainted with both Adam and Noah.

44. From the foregoing it is easily to be seen, not only how the knowledge of God came into the world, but upon what principle it was preserved; that from the time it was first communicated, it was retained in the minds of righteous men, who taught not only their own posterity but the world; so that there was no need of a new revelation to man, after Adam's creation to Noah, to give them the first idea or notion of the existence of a God; and not only of a God, but the true and living God.

45. Having traced the chronology of the world from Adam to Noah, we will now trace it from Noah to Abraham. Noah was 502 years old when Shem was born; 98 years afterwards the flood came, being the 600th year of Noah's age. And Moses informs us that Noah lived after the flood 350 years, making him 950 years old when he died. Genesis ix. 28, 29.

46. Shem was 100 years old when Arphaxad was born. Genesis xi. 10. Arphaxad was 35 when Salah was born (xi. 12): Salah was 30 when Eber was born (xi. 14); Eber was 34 when Peleg was born, in whose days the earth was divided (xi 16); Peleg was 30 when Reu was born (xi. 18); Reu was 32 when

Serug was born (xi. 20) ; Serug was 30 when Nahor was born (xi. 22) ; Nahor was 29 when Terah was born (xi. 24) ; Terah was 70 when Haran and Abraham were born (xi. 26).

47. There is some difficulty in the account given by Moses of Abraham's birth. Some have supposed that Abraham was not born until Terah was 130 years old. This conclusion is drawn from a variety of scriptures, which are not to our purpose at present to quote. Neither is it a matter of any consequence to us whether Abraham was born when Terah was 70 years old, or 130. But in order that there may no doubt exist upon any mind in relation to the object lying immediately before us, in presenting the present chronology we will date the birth of Abraham at the latest period, that is, when Terah was 130 years old. It appears from this account that from the flood to the birth of Abraham, was 352 years.

48. Moses informs us that Shem lived after he begat Arphaxad, 500 years (xi. 11) ; this added to 100 years, which was his age when Arphaxad was born, makes him 600 years old when he died. Arphaxad lived, after he begat Salah, 403 years (xi. 13) ; this added to 35 years, which was his age when Salah was born, makes him 438 years old when he died. Salah lived after he begat Eber, 403 years (xi. 15) ; this added to 30 years, which was his age when Eber was born, makes him 433 years old when he died. Eber lived after he begat Peleg, 430 years (xi. 17) ; this added to 34 years, which was his age when Peleg was born, makes him 464 years old. Peleg lived after he begat Reu, 209 years (xi. 19) ; this added to 30 years, which was his age when Reu was born makes him 239 years old when he died. Reu lived after he begat Serug 207 years (xi. 21) ; this added to 32 years, which was his age when Serug was born, makes him 239 years old when he died. Serug lived after he begat Nahor, 200 years (xi. 23) ; this added to 30 years, which was his age when Nahor was born, makes him 230 years old when he died. Nahor lived after he begat Terah, 119 years (xi. 25) ; this added to 29 years, which was his age when Terah was born, makes him 148 years when he died. Terah was 130 years old when Abraham was born, and is supposed to have lived 75 years after his birth, making him 205 years old when he died.

49. Agreeable to this last account, Peleg died in the 1996th year of the world, Nahor in the 1997th, and Noah in the 2006th. So that Peleg, in whose days the earth was divided, and Nahor,

the grandfather of Abraham, both died before Noah—the former being 239 years old, and the latter 148; and who cannot but see that they must have had a long and intimate acquaintance with Noah?

50. Rue died in the 2026th year of the world, Serug in the 2049th, Terah in the 2083rd, Arphaxad in the 2096th, Salah in the 2126th, Shem in the 2158th, Abraham in the 2183rd, and Eber in the 2187th, which was four years after Abraham's death. And Eber was the fourth from Noah.

51. Nahor, Abraham's brother, was 58 years old when Noah died, Terah 128, Serug 187, Reu 219, Eber 283, Salah 313, Arphaxad 344, and Shem 448.

52. It appears from this account, that Nahor, brother of Abraham, Terah, Nahor, Serug, Reu, Peleg, Eber, Salah, Arphaxad, Shem, and Noah, all lived on the earth at the same time; and that Abraham was 18 years old when Reu died, 41 when Serug and his brother Nahor died, 75 when Terah died, 88 when Arphaxad died, 118 when Salah died, 150 when Shem died, and that Eber lived four years after Abraham's death. And that Shem, Arphaxad, Salah, Eber, Reu, Serug, Terah, and Nahor, the brother of Abraham, and Abraham, lived at the same time. And that Nahor, brother of Abraham, Terah, Serug, Reu, Eber, Salah, Arphaxad, and Shem, were all acquainted with both Noah and Abraham.

53. We have now traced the chronology of the world agreeable to the account given in our present Bible, from Adam to Abraham, and have clearly determined, beyond the power of controversy, that there was no difficulty in preserving the knowledge of God in the world from the creation of Adam, and the manifestation made to his immediate descendents, as set forth in the former part of this lecture; so that the students in this class need not have any doubt resting on their minds on this subject, for they can easily see that it is impossible for it to be otherwise, but that the knowledge of the existence of a God must have continued from father to son, as a matter of tradition at least; for we cannot suppose that a knowledge of this important fact could have existed in the mind of any of the beforementioned individuals, without their having made it known to their posterity.

54. We have now shown how it was that the first thought ever existed in the mind of any individual that there was such

a Being as a God, who had created and did uphold all things:
that it was by reason of the manifestation which he first made to
our father Adam, when he stood in his presence, and conversed
with him face to face, at the time of his creation.

55. Let us here observe, that after any portion of the
human family are made acquainted with the important fact that
there is a God, who has created and does uphold all things, the
extent of their knowledge respecting his character and glory
will depend upon their diligence and faithfulness in seeking
after him, until, like Enoch, the brother of Jared, and Moses,
they shall obtain faith in God, and power with him to behold
him face to face.

56. We have now clearly set forth how it is, and how it
was, that God became an object of faith for rational beings;
and also, upon what foundation the testimony was based which
excited the inquiry and diligent search of the ancient saints to
seek after and obtain a knowledge of the glory of God; and we
have seen that it was human testimony, and human testimony
only, that excited this inquiry, in the first instance, in their
minds. It was the credence they gave to the testimony of their
fathers, this testimony having aroused their minds to inquire
after the knowledge of God; the inquiry frequently terminated,
indeed always terminated when rightly pursued, in the most
glorious discoveries and eternal certainty.

QUESTIONS AND ANSWERS ON THE FOREGOING PRINCIPLES

Is there a being who has faith in himself, independently?
There is.

Who is it? It is God.

How do you prove that God has faith in himself independently? Because he is omnipotent, omnipresent, and omniscient;
without beginning of days or end of life, and in him all fullness
dwells. Ephesians i. 23: "Which is his body, the fullness of him
that filleth all in all." Colossians i. 19: "For it pleased the Father
that in him should all fullness dwell." Lecture ii. 2.

Is he the object in whom the faith of all other rational and
accountable beings center, for life and salvation? He is.

How do you prove it? Isaiah xlv. 22: "Look unto me and be
ye saved, all the ends of the earth; for I am God, and there is
none else." Romans xi. 34, 35, 36: "For who hath known the
mind of the Lord; or who hath been his counselor? or who

hath first given to him, and it shall be recompensed unto him again? For of him, and through him, and to him, are all things, to whom be glory for ever. Amen." Isaiah xl., from the 9th to the 18th verses: "O Zion, that bringest good tidings; (or, O thou that tellest good tidings to Zion) get thee up into the high mountain; O Jerusalem, that bringest good tidings; (or, O thou that tellest good tidings to Jerusalem) lift up thy voice with strength; lift it up, be not afraid; say unto the cities of Judah, Behold your God! Behold the Lord your God will come with strong hand (or, against the strong); and his arm shall rule for him; behold, his reward is with him, and his work before him (or, recompense for his work). He shall feed his flock like a shepherd; he shall gather his lambs with his arms, and carry them in his bosom, and shall gently lead those that are with young. Who hath measured the waters in the hollow of his hand, and meted out heaven with the span, and comprehended the dust of the earth in a measure, weighed the mountains in scales, and the hills in a balance? Who hath directed the Spirit of the Lord, or, being his counselor, hath taught him? With whom took he counsel, and who instructed him and taught him in the past of judgment, and taught him knowledge and showed to him the way of understanding? Behold, the nations are as a drop of a bucket and are counted as the small dust of the balance: behold, he taketh up the isles as a very little thing. And Lebanon is not sufficient to burn, nor the beast thereof sufficient for a burnt offering. All nations are before him as nothing, and they are counted to him less than nothing, and vanity." Jeremiah li. 15, 16: "He (the Lord) hath made the earth by his power, he hath established the world by his wisdom, and hath stretched out the heaven by his understanding. When he uttereth his voice there is a multitude of waters in the heavens, and he causeth the vapors to ascend from the ends of the earth; he maketh light-nings with rain, and bringeth forth the wind out of his treasures. 1 Corinthians viii. 6: "But to us there is but one God, the Father, of whom are all things, and we in him; and one Lord Jesus Christ by whom are all things, and we by him." Lecture ii. 2

How did men first come to the knowledge of the existence of a God, so as to exercise faith in him? In order to answer this question, it will be necessary to go back and examine man at his creation; the circumstances in which he was placed, and the knowledge which he had of God. Lecture ii. 3, 4, 5, 6,

7, 8, 9, 10, 11. First, when man was created he stood in the
presence of God. Genesis i. 27, 28. From this we learn that
man, at his creation, stood in the presence of his God, and had
most perfect knowledge of his existence. Secondly, God conversed with him after his transgression. Genesis iii. from the
8th to the 22nd. Lecture ii. 13, 14, 15, 16, 17. From this we
learn that, though man did transgress, he was not deprived
of the previous knowledge which he had of the existence of
God. Lecture ii. 19. Thirdly, God conversed with man after
he cast him out of the garden. Lecture ii. 22, 23, 24, 25. Fourthly, God also conversed with Cain after he had slain Abel. Genesis
iv. from the 4th to the 6th. Lecture ii. 26, 27, 28, 29.

What is the object of the foregoing quotation? It is that it
may be clearly seen how it was that the first thoughts were
suggested to the minds of men of the existence of God, and how
extensively this knowledge was spread among the immediate
descendants of Adam. Lecture ii. 30, 31, 32, 33.

What testimony had the immediate descendents of Adam,
in proof of the existence of God? The testimony of their father.
And after they were made acquainted with his existence, by the
testimony of their father, they were dependent upon the exercise
of their own faith, for a knowledge of his character, perfections,
and attributes. Lecture ii. 23, 24, 25, 26.

Had any other of the human family, besides Adam, a knowledge of the existence of God, in the first instance, by any other
means than human testimony? They had not. For previous to
the time that they could have power to obtain a manifestation
for themselves, the all-important fact had been communicated
to them by their common father; and so from father to child
the knowledge was communicated as extensively as the knowledge of his existence was known; for it was by this means, in
the first instance, that men had a knowledge of his existence.
Lecture ii. 35, 36.

How do you know that the knowledge of the existence of
God was communicated in this manner, throughout the different
ages of the world? By the chronology obtained through the
revelations of God.

How would you divide that chronology in order to convey
it to the understanding clearly? Into two parts—First, by em-
bracing that period of the world from Adam to Noah; and
secondly, from Noah to Abraham; from which period the

knowledge of the existence of God has been so general that it is a matter of no dispute in what manner the idea of his existence has been retained in the world.

How many noted righteous men lived from Adam to Noah? Nine; which includes Abel, who was slain by his brother.

What are their names? Abel, Seth, Enos, Cainan, Mahalaleel, Jared, Enoch, Methuselah, and Lamech.

How old was Adam when Seth was born? One hundred and thirty years. Genesis v. 3.

How many years did Adam live after Seth was born? Eight hundred. Genesis v. 4.

How old was Adam when he died? Nine hundred and thirty years. Genesis v. 5.

How old was Seth when Enos was born? One hundred and five years. Genesis v. 6.

How old was Enos when Cainan was born? Ninety years. Genesis v. 9.

How old was Cainan when Mahalaleel was born? Seventy years. Genesis v. 12.

How old was Mahalaleel when Jared was born? Sixty-five years. Genesis v. 15.

How old was Jared when Enoch was born? One hundred and sixty-two years. Genesis v. 18.

How old was Enoch when Methuselah was born? Sixty-five years. Genesis v. 21.

How old was Methuselah when Lamech was born? One hundred and eighty-seven years. Genesis v. 25.

How old was Lamech when Noah was born? One hundred and eighty-two years. Genesis v. 28. For this chronology, see Lecture ii. 37.

How many years, according to this account, was it from Adam to Noah? One thousand and fifty-six years.

How old was Lamech when Adam died? Lamech, the ninth from Adam (including Abel), and father of Noah, was fifty-six years old when Adam died.

How old was Methuselah? Two hundred and forty-three years.

How old was Enoch? Three hundred and eight years.

How old was Jared? Four hundred and seventy years.

How old was Mahalaleel? Five hundred and thirty-five years.

How old was Cainan? Six hundred and five years.

How old was Enos? Six hundred and ninety-five years.

How old was Seth? Eight hundred years. For this item of the account, see lecture ii. 38.

How many of these noted men were cotemporary with Adam? Nine.

What are their names? Abel, Seth, Enos, Cainan, Mahalaleel, Jared, Enoch, Methuselah and Lamech. Lecture ii. 39.

How long did Seth live after Enos was born? Eight hundred and seven years. Genesis v. 7.

What was Seth's age when he died? Nine hundred and twelve years. Genesis v. 8.

How long did Enos live after Cainan was born? Eight hundred and fifteen years. Genesis v. 10.

What was Enos's age when he died? Nine hundred and five years. Genesis v. 11.

How long did Cainan live after Mahalaleel was born? Eight hundred and forty years. Genesis v. 13.

What was Cainan's age when he died? Nine hnudred and ten years. Genesis v. 14.

How long did Mahalaleel live after Jared was born? Eight hundred and thirty years. Genesis v. 16.

What was Mahalaleel's age when he died? Eight hundred and ninety-five years. Genesis v. 17.

How long did Jared live after Enoch was born? Eight hundred years. Genesis v. 19.

What was Jared's age when he died? Nine hundred and sixty-two years. Genesis v. 20.

How long did Enoch walk with God after Methuselah was born? Three hundred years. Genesis v. 22.

What was Enoch's age when he was translated? Three hundred and sixty-five years. Genesis v. 23.*

*For Enoch's age, see Covenants and Commandments, Section 107. 49.

How long did Methuselah live after Lamech was born? Seven hundred and eighty-two years. Genesis v. 26.

What was Methuselah's age when he died? Nine hundred and sixty-nine years. Genesis v. 27.

How long did Lamech live after Noah was born? Five hundred and ninety-five years. Genesis v. 30.

What was Lamech's age when he died? Seven hundred and seventy-seven years. Genesis v. 31. For the account of the last item see lecture ii. 40.

In what year of the world did Adam die? In the nine hundred and thirtieth.

In what year was Enoch translated?* In the nine hundred and eighty-seventh.

In what year did Seth die? In one thousand and forty-second.

In what year did Enos die? In the eleven hundred and fortieth.

In what year did Cainan die? In the twelve hundred and thirty-fifth.

In what year did Mahalaleel die? In the twelve hundred and ninetieth.

In what year did Jared die? In the fourteen hundred and twenty-second.

In what year did Lamech die? In the sixteen hundred and fifty-first.

In what year did Methuselah die? In the sixteen hundred and fifty-sixth. For this account see lecture ii. 41.

How old was Noah when Enos died? Eighty-four years.

How old when Cainan died? One hundred and seventy-nine years.

How old when Mahalaleel died? Two hundred and thirty-four years.

How old when Jared died? Three hundred and sixty-six years.

How old when Lamech died? Five hundred and ninety-five years.

How old when Methuselah died? Six hundred years. See lecture ii. 42, for the last item.

How many of those men lived in the days of Noah? Six.

What are their names? Enos, Cainan, Mahalaleel, Jared, Methuselah, and Lamech. Lecture ii. 43.

How many of those men were cotemporary with Adam and Noah both? Six.

What are their names? Enos, Cainan, Mahalaleel, Jared, Methuselah, and Lamech. Lecture ii. 43.

According to the foregoing account how was the knowledge of the existence of God first suggested to the minds of men? By the manifestation made to our father Adam, when he was in the presence of God, both before and while he was in Eden. Lecture ii. 44.

How was the knowledge of the existence of God disseminated among the inhabitants of the world? By tradition from father to son. Lecture ii. 44.

How old was Noah when Shem was born? Five hundred and two years. Genesis v. 32.

What was the term of years from the birth of Shem to the flood? Ninety-eight.

What was the term of years that Noah lived after the flood? Three hundred and fifty. Genesis ix. 28.

What was Noah's age when he died? Nine hundred and fifty years. Genesis ix. 29. Lecture ii. 45.

What was Shem's age when Arphaxad was born? One hundred years. Genesis xi. 10.

What was Arphaxad's age when Salah was born? Thirty-five years. Genesis xi. 12.

What was Salah's age when Eber was born? Thirty years. Genesis xi. 16.

What was Eber's age when Peleg was born? Thirty-four years. Genesis xi. 14.

What was Peleg's age when Reu was born? Thirty years. Genesis xi. 18.

What was Reu's age when Serug was born? Thirty-two years. Genesis xi. 20.

What was Serug's age when Nahor was born? Thirty years. Genesis xi. 22.

What was Nahor's age when Terah was born? Twenty-nine years. Genesis xi. 24.

What was Terah's age when Nahor (the father of Abraham) was born? Seventy years. Genesis xi, 26.

What was Terah's age when Abraham was born? Some suppose one hundred and thirty years, and others seventy. Genesis xi. 26. Lecture ii. 46.

What was the number of years from the flood to the birth of Abraham? Supposing Abraham to have been born when Terah was one hundred and thirty years old, it was three hundred and fifty-two years: but if he was born when Terah was seventy years old, it was two hundred and ninety-two years. Lecture ii. 47.

How long did Shem live after Arphaxad was born? Five hundred years. Genesis xi. 11.

What was Shem's age when he died? Six hundred years. Genesis xi. 11.

What number of years did Arphaxad live after Salah was born? Four hundred and three years. Genesis xi. 13.

What was Arphaxad's age when he died? Four hundred and thirty-three years.

What number of years did Eber live after Peleg was born? Four hundred and three years.

What was Salah's age when he died? Four hundred and thirty-three years.

What number of years did Eber live after Peleg was born? Four hundred and thirty years. Genesis xi. 17.

What was Eber's age when he died? Four hundred and sixty-four years.

What number of years did Peleg live after Reu was born? Two hundred and nine years. Genesis xi. 19.

What was Peleg's age when he died? Two hundred and thirty-nine years.

What number of years did Reu live after Serug was born? Two hundred and seven years. Genesis xi. 21.

What was Reu's age when he died? Two hundred and thirty-nine years.

What number of years did Serug live after Nahor was born? Two hundred years. Genesis xi. 23.

What was Serug's age when he died? Two hundred and thirty years.

What number of years did Nahor live after Terah was born? One hundred and nineteen years. Genesis xi. 25.

What was Nahor's age when he died? One hundred and forty-eight years.

What number of years did Terah live after Abraham was born? Supposing Terah to have been one hundred and thirty years old when Abraham was born, he lived seventy-five years; but if Abraham was born when Terah was seventy-five years old, he lived one hundred and thirty-five.

What was Terah's age when he died? Two hundred and five years. Genesis xi. 32. For this account, from the birth of Arphaxad to the death of Terah, see lecture ii. 48.

In what year of the world did Peleg die? Agreeable to the foregoing chronology, he died in the nineteen hundred and ninety-sixth year of the world.

In what year of the world did Nahor die? In the nineteen hundred and ninety-seventh.

In what year of the world did Noah die? In the two thousand and sixth.

In what year of the world did Reu die? In the two thousand and twenty-sixth.

In what year of the world did Serug die? In the two thousand and forty-ninth.

In what year of the world did Terah die? In the two thousand and eighty-third.

In what year of the world did Arphaxad die? In the two thousand and ninety-sixth

In what year of the world did Salah die? In the twenty-one hundred and twenty-sixth.

In what year of the world did Abraham die? In the twenty-one hundred and eighty-third.

In what year of the world did Eber die? In the twenty-one hundred and eighty-seventh. For this account of the year of the world in which those men died, see lecture ii. 49, 50.

How old was Nahor (Abraham's brother) when Noah died? Fifty-eight years.

How old was Terah? One hundred and twenty-eight.

How old was Serug? One hundred and eighty-seven.

How old was Reu? Two hundred and nineteen.

How old was Eber? Two hundred and eighty-three.

How old was Salah? Three hundred and thirteen.

How old was Arphaxad? Three hundred and fory-eight.

How old was Shem? Four hundred and forty-eight.

For the last account see lecture ii. 51.

How old was Abraham when Reu died? Eighteen years, if he was born when Terah was one hundred and thirty years old.

What was his age when Serug and Nahor (Abraham's brother) died? Forty-one years.

What was his age when Terah died? Seventy-five years.

What was his age when Arphaxad died? Eighty-eight.

What was his age when Salah died? One hundred and eighteen years.

What was his age when Shem died? One hundred and fifty years. For this see lecture ii. 52.

How many noted characters lived from Noah to Abraham? Ten.

What are their names? Shem, Arphaxad, Salah, Eber,

Peleg, Reu, Serug, Nahor, Terah, and Nahor, (Abraham's brother). Lecture ii. 52.

How many of these were cotemporary with Noah? The whole.

How many with Abraham? Eight.

What are their names? Nahor (Abraham's brother) Terah, Serug, Reu, Eber, Salah, Arphaxad, and Shem. Lecture ii. 52.

How many were cotemporary with both Noah and Abraham? Eight.

What are their names? Shem, Arphaxad, Salah, Eber, Reu, Serug, Terah, and Nahor (Abraham's brother). Lecture ii. 52.

Did any of these men die before Noah? They did.

Who were they? Peleg, in whose days the earth was divided, and Nahor, (Abraham's grandfather). Lecture ii. 49.

Did any one of them live longer than Abraham? There was one. Lecture ii. 50.

Who was he? Eber, the fourth from Noah. Lecture ii. 50.

In whose days was the earth divided? In the days of Peleg.

Where have we the account given that the earth was divided in the days of Peleg? Genesis x. 25.

Can you repeat the sentence? "Unto Eber were born two sons: the name of one was Peleg, for in his days the earth was divided."

What testimony have men, in the first instance, that there is a God? Human testimony, and human testimony only. Lecture ii. 56.

What excited the ancient saints to seek diligently after a knowledge of the glory of God, his perfections and attributes? The credence they gave to the testimony of their fathers. Lecture ii. 56.

How do men obtain a knowledge of the glory of God, his perfections and attributes? By devoting themselves to his service, through prayer and supplication incessantly strengthening their faith in him, until, like Enoch, the brother of Jared, and Moses, they obtain a manifestation of God to themselves. Lecture ii. 55.

Is the knowledge of the existence of God a matter of mere tradition, founded upon human testimony alone, until persons receive a manifestation of God to themselves? It is.

How do you prove it? From the whole of the first and second lectures.

LECTURE THIRD

1. In the second lecture it was shewn how it was that the knowledge of the existence of God came into the world, and by what means the first thoughts were suggested to the minds of men that such a Being did actually exist; and that it was by reason of the knowledge of his existence that there was a foundation laid for the exercise of faith in him, as the only Being in whom faith could center for life and salvation; for faith could not center in a Being of whose existence we have no idea, because the idea of his existence in the first instance is essential to the exercise of faith in him. Romans x. 14: "How then shall they call on him in whom they have not believed? and how shall they believe in him of whom they have not heard? and how shall they hear without a preacher (or one sent to tell them)? So, then, faith comes by hearing the word of God." (New Translation).

2. Let us here observe, that three things are necessary in order that any rational and intelligent being may exercise faith in God unto life and salvation.

3. First, the idea that he actually exists.

4. Secondly, a *correct* idea of his character, perfections, and attributes.

5. Thirdly, an actual knowledge that the course of life which he is pursuing is according to his will. For without an acquaintance with these three important facts, the faith of every rational being must be imperfect and unproductive; but with this understanding it can become perfect and fruitful, abounding in righteousness, unto the praise and glory of God the Father, and the Lord Jesus Christ.

6. Having previously been made acquainted with the way the idea of his existence came into the world, as well as the fact of his existence, we shall proceed to examine his character, perfections, and attributes, in order that this class may see, not only the just grounds which they have for the exercise of faith in him for life and salvation, but the reasons that all the world, also, as far as the idea of his existence extends, may have to exercise faith in him, the Father of all living.

7. As we have been indebted to a revelation which God made of himself to his creatures, in the first instance, for the idea of his existence, so in like manner we are indebted to the

2

revelations which he has given to us for a correct understanding of his character, perfections, and attributes; because without the revelations which he has given to us, no man by searching could find out God. Job. xi. 7, 8, 9. 1 Corinthians ii. 9, 10, 11. "But as it is written, eye hath not seen, nor ear heard, neither have entered into the heart of man, the things which God hath prepared for them that love him; but God hath revealed them unto us by his Spirit, for the Spirit searcheth all things, yea, the deep things of God. For what man knoweth the things of a man, save the spirit of man which is in him? Even so, the things of God knoweth no man but the Spirit of God."

8. Having said so much we proceed to examine the character which the revelations have given of God.

9. Moses gives us the following account in Exodus, xxxiv. 6: "And the Lord passed by before him, and proclaimed, 'The Lord God, the Lord God, merciful and gracious, long-suffering and abundant in goodness and truth.'" Psalm ciii. 6, 7, 8: "The Lord executeth righteousness and judgment for all that are oppressed. He made known his ways unto Moses, his acts unto the children of Israel. The Lord is merciful and gracious, slow to anger and plenteous in mercy." Psalm ciii. 17, 18: "But the mercy of the Lord is from everlasting to everlasting upon them that fear him, and his righteousness unto children's children, to such as keep his covenant, and to those that remember his commandments to do them." Psalm xc. 2: "Before the mountains were brought forth, or ever thou hadst formed the earth and the world, even from everlasting to everlasting thou art God." Hebrews i. 10, 11, 12: And thou, Lord, in the beginning, hast laid the foundation of the earth; and the heavens are the works of thine hands: they shall perish, but thou remainest; and they all shall wax old as doth a garment; and as a vesture shalt thou fold them up, and they shall be changed; but thou art the same and thy years shall not fail." James i. 17: "Every good gift and every perfect gift is from above, and cometh down from the Father of lights, with whom is no variableness, neither shadow of turning." Malachi iii. 6: "For I am the Lord, I change not; therefore ye sons of Jacob are not consumed."

10. Book of Commandments, Sec. 3, v. 2: "For God does not walk in crooked paths, neither does he turn to the right hand or the left, or vary from that which he has said, therefore his paths are straight, and his course is one eternal round." Book

of Commandments, Sec. 35, v. 1: "Listen to the voice of the Lord your God, even Alpha and Omega, the beginning and the end, whose course is one eternal round, the same yesterday, to-day, and forever."

11. Numbers xxiii. 19: "God is not a man that he should lie, neither the son of man that he should repent." 1 John iv. 8: "He that loveth not, knoweth not God, for God is love." Acts x. 34, 35: "Then Peter opened his mouth and said, 'Of a truth I perceive that God is no respecter of persons, but in every nation he that feareth God and worketh righteousness is accepted with him.'"

12. From the foregoing testimonies we learn the following things respecting the character of God:

13. First, that he was God before the world was created, and the same God that he was after it was created.

14. Secondly, that he is merciful and gracious, slow to anger, abundant in goodness, and that he was so from everlasting, and will be to everlasting.

15. Thirdly, that he changes not, neither is there variableness with him; but that he is the same from everlasting to everlasting, being the same yesterday, to-day, and for ever; and that his course is one eternal round, without variation.

16. Fourthly, that he is a God of truth and cannot lie.

17. Fifthly, that he is no respecter of persons: but in every nation he that fears God and works righteousness is accepted of him.

18. Sixthly, that he is love.

19. An acquaintance with these attributes in the divine character, is essentially necessary, in order that the faith of any rational being can center in him for life and salvation. For if he did not, in the first instance, believe him to be God, that is, the Creator and upholder of all things, he could not *center* his faith in him for life and salvation, for fear there should be greater than he who would thwart all his plans, and he like the gods of the heathen, would be unable to fulfill his promises; but seeing he is God over all, from everlasting to everlasting, the Creator and upholder of all things, no such fear can exist in the minds of those who put their trust in him, so that in this respect their faith can be without wavering.

20. But secondly; unless he was merciful and gracious, slow to anger, long-suffering and full of goodness, such is the

weakness of human nature, and so great the frailties and imperfections of men, that unless they believed that these excellencies existed in the divine character, the faith necessary to salvation could not exist; for doubt would take the place of faith, and those who know their weakness and liability to sin would be in constant doubt of salvation if it were not for the idea which they have of the excellency of the character of God, that he is slow to anger and long-suffering, and of a forgiving disposition, and does forgive iniquity, transgression, and sin. An idea of these facts does away doubt, and makes faith exceedingly strong.

21. But it is equally as necessary that men should have the idea that he is a God who changes not, in order to have faith in him, as it is to have the idea that he is gracious and long-suffering; for without the idea of unchangeableness in the character of the Deity, doubt would take the place of faith. But with the idea that he changes not, faith lays hold upon the excellencies in his character with unshaken confidence, believing he is the same yesterday, to-day, and forever, and that his course is one eternal round.

22. And again, the idea that he is a God of truth and cannot lie, is equally as necessary to the exercise of faith in him as the idea of his unchangeableness. For without the idea that he was a God of truth and could not lie, the confidence necessary to be placed in his word in order to the exercise of faith in him could not exist. But having the idea that he is not man, that he cannot lie, it gives power to the minds of men to exercise faith in him.

23. But it is also necessary that men should have an idea that he is no respecter of persons, for with the idea of all the other excellencies in his character, and this one wanting, men could not exercise faith in him; because if he were a respecter of persons, they could not tell what their privileges were, nor how far they were authorized to exercise faith in him, or whether they were authorized to do it at all, but all must be confusion; but no sooner are the minds of men made acquainted with the truth on this point, that he is no respecter of persons, than they see that they have authority by faith to lay hold on eternal life, the richest boon of heaven, because God is no respecter of persons, and that every man in every nation has an equal privilege.

24. And lastly, but not less important to the exercise of faith in God, is the idea that he is love; for with all the other

excellencies in his character, without this one to influence them, they could not have such powerful dominion over the minds of men; but when the idea is planted in the mind that he is love, who cannot see the just ground that men of every nation, kindred, and tongue, have to exercise faith in God so as to obtain eternal life?

25. From the above description of the character of the Deity, which is given him in the revelations to men, there is a sure foundation for the exercise of faith in him among every people, nation, and kindred, from age to age, and from generation to generation.

26. Let us here observe that the foregoing is the character which is given of God in his revelations to the Former-day Saints, and it is also the character which is given of him in his revelations to the Latter-day Saints, so that the saints of former days and those of latter days are both alike in this respect; the Latter-day Saints having as good grounds to exercise faith in God as the Former-day Saints had, because the same character is given of him to both.

QUESTIONS AND ANSWERS ON THE FOREGOING PRINCIPLES

What was shown in the second lecture? It was shown how the knowledge of the existence of God came into the world. Lecture iii. 1.

What is the effect of the idea of his existence among men? It lays the foundation for the exercise of faith in him. Lecture iii. 1.

Is the idea of his existence, in the first instance, necessary in order for the exercise of faith in him? It is. Lecture iii. 1.

How do you prove it? By the tenth chapter of Romans and fourteenth verse. Lecture iii. 1.

How many things are necessary for us to understand, respecting the Deity and our relation to him, in order that we may exercise faith in him for life and salvation? Three. Lecture iii. 2.

What are they? First, that God does actually exist; secondly, correct ideas of his character, his perfections and attributes; and thirdly, that the course which we pursue is according to his mind and will. Lecture iii. 3, 4, 5.

Would the idea of any one or two of the above-mentioned things enable a person to exercise faith in God? It would not, for without the idea of them all faith would be imperfect and unproductive. Lecture iii. 5.

Would an idea of these three things lay a sure foundation for the exercise of faith in God, so as to obtain life and salvation? It would; for by the idea of these three things, faith could become perfect and fruitful, abounding in righteousness unto the praise and glory of God. Lecture iii. 5.

How are we to be made acquainted with the before-mentioned things respecting the Deity, and respecting ourselves? By revelation. Lecture iii. 6.

Could these things be found out by any other means than by revelation? They could not.

How do you prove it? By the scriptures. Job xi. 7, 8, 9. 1 Corinthians ii. 9, 10, 11. Lecture iii. 7.

What things do we learn in the revelations of God respecting his character? We learn the six following things: First, that he was God before the world was created, and the same God that he was after it was created. Secondly, that he is merciful and gracious, slow to anger, abundant in goodness, and that he was so from everlasting, and will be so to everlasting. Thirdly, that he changes not, neither is there variableness with him, and that his course is one eternal round. Fourthly, that he is a God of truth, and cannot lie. Fifthly, that he is no respecter of persons; and sixthly, that he is love. Lecture iii. 12, 13, 14, 15, 16, 17, 18.

Where do you find the revelations which gives us this idea of the character of the Deity? In the Bible and Book of Commandments, and they are quoted in the third lecture. Lecture iii. 9, 10, 11.

What effect would it have on any rational being not to have an idea that the Lord was God, the Creator and upholder of all things? It would prevent him from exercising faith in him unto life and salvation.

Why would it prevent him from exercising faith in God? Because he would be as the heathen, not knowing but there he might be a being greater and more powerful than he, and thereby be prevented from filling his promises. Lecture iii. 19.

Does this idea prevent this doubt? It does; for persons having this idea are enabled thereby to exercise faith without this doubt. Lecture iii. 19.

Is it not also necessary to have the idea that God is merciful and gracious, long-suffering and full of goodness? It is. Lecture iii. 20.

Why is it necessary? Because of the weakness and imperfections of human nature, and the great frailties of man; for such is the weakness of man, and such his frailties, that he is liable to sin continually, and if God were not long-suffering, and full of compassion, gracious and merciful, and of a forgiving disposition, man would be cut off from before him, in consequence of which he would be in continual doubt and could not exercise faith; for where doubt is, there faith has no power; but by man's believing that God is full of compassion and forgiveness, long-suffering and slow to anger, he can exercise faith in him and overcome doubt, so as to be exceedingly strong. Lecture iii. 20.

Is it not equally as necessary that man should have an idea that God changes not, neither is there variableness with him, in order to exercise faith in him unto life and salvation? It is; because without this, he would not know how soon the mercy of God might change into cruelty, his long-suffering into rashness, his love into hatred, and in consequence of which doubt man would be incapable of exercising faith in him, but having the idea that he is unchangeable, man can have faith in him continually, believing that what he was yesterday he is to-day, and will be forever. Lecture iii. 21.

Is it not necessary also, for men to have an idea that God is a being of truth before they can have perfect faith in him? It is; for unless men have this idea they cannot place confidence in his word, and, not being able to place confidence in his word, they could not have faith in him; but believing that he is a God of truth, and that his word cannot fail, their faith can rest in him without doubt Lecture iii. 22.

Could man exercise faith in God so as to obtain eternal life unless he believed that God was no respecter of persons? He could not; because without this idea he could not certainly know that it was his privilege so to do, and in consequence of this doubt his faith could not be sufficiently strong to save him. Lecture iii. 23.

Would it be possible for a man to exercise faith in God, so as to be saved, unless he had an idea that God was love? He could not; because man could not love God unless he had an idea that

God was love, and if he did not love God he could not have faith in him. Lecture iii. 24.

What is the description which the sacred writers give of the character of the Deity calculated to do? It is calculated to lay a foundation for the exercise of faith in him, as far as the knowledge extends, among all people, tongues, languages, kindreds and nations, and that from age to age, and from generation to generation. Lecture iii. 25.

Is the character which God has given of himself uniform? It is, in all his revelations, whether to the Former-day Saints, or to the Latter-day Saints, so that they all have the authority to exercise faith in him, and to expect, by the exercise of their faith, to enjoy the same blessings. Lecture iii. 26.

The Following Excerpt Is Not A Part of The Lectures On Faith

There are but a very few beings in the world who understand rightly the character of God. The great majority of mankind do not comprehend anything, either that which is past, or that which is to come, as it respects their relationship to God. They do not know, neither do they understand the nature of that relationship and consequently they know but little above the brute beast, or more than to eat, drink and sleep. This is all man knows about God or his existence, unless it is given by the inspiration of the Almighty.

If a man learns nothing more than to eat, drink and sleep, and does not comprehend any of the designs of God, the beast comprehends the same things. It eats, drinks, sleeps, and knows nothing more about God; yet it knows as much as we, unless we are able to comprehend by the inspiration of Almighty God. If men do not comprehend the character of God, they do not comprehend themselves. I want to go back to the beginning, and so lift your minds into a more lofty sphere and a more exalted understanding than what the human mind generally aspires to. "King Follett" discourse, by Joseph the Prophet. See *The Vision*, pp. 15-16.

LECTURE FOURTH

1. Having shown, in the third lecture, that correct ideas of the character of God are necessary in order to the exercise of faith in him unto life and salvation; and that without correct ideas of his character the minds of men could not have sufficient power with God to the exercise of faith necessary to the enjoyment of eternal life; and that correct ideas of his character lay a foundation, as far as his character is concerned, for the exercise of faith, so as to enjoy the fullness of the blessing of the gospel of Jesus Christ even that of eternal glory; we shall now proceed to show the connection there is between correct ideas of the attributes of God, and the exercise of faith in him unto eternal life.

2. Let us here observe, that the real design which the God of heaven had in view in making the human family acquainted with his attributes, was, that they, through the ideas of the existence of his attributes, might be enabled to exercise faith in him, and through the exercise of faith in him, might obtain eternal life; for without the idea of the existence of the attributes which belong to God, the minds of men could not have power to exercise faith in him so as to lay hold upon eternal life. The God of heaven, understanding most perfectly the constitution of human nature, and the weakness of men, knew what was necessary to be revealed, and what ideas must be planted in their minds in order that they might be enabled to exercise faith in him unto eternal life.

3. Having said so much, we shall proceed to examine the attributes of God, as set forth in his revelations to the human family, and to show how necessary correct ideas of his attributes are to enable men to exercise faith in him; for without these ideas being planted in the minds of men it would be out of the power of any person or persons to exercise faith in God so as to obtain eternal life. So that the divine communications made to men in the first instance were designed to establish in their minds the ideas necessary to enable them to exercise faith in God, and through this means to be partakers of his glory.

4. We have, in the revelations which he has given to the human family, the following account of his attributes:

5. First—Knowledge. Acts xv. 18: "Known unto God are

all his works from the beginning of the world," Isaiah xlvi. 9,
10: "Remember the former things of old: for I am God, and
there is none else; I am God, and there is none like me, *declaring
the end from the beginning,* and from ancient time the things
that are not yet done, saying 'My counsel shall stand, and I will
do all my pleasure.' "

6. Secondly—Faith or power. Hebrews xi 3: "Through
faith we understand that the worlds were framed by the word of
God." Genesis i. 1: "In the beginning God created the heaven
and the earth." Isaiah xiv. 24, 27: "The Lord of hosts hath
sworn, saying, 'Surely as I have thought, so shall it come to pass:
and as I have purposed so shall it stand. For the Lord of Hosts
hath purposed, and who shall disannul it? and his hand is
stretched out, and who shall turn it back?' "

7. Thirdly—Justice. Psalm lxxxix. 14: "Justice and judgment are the habitation of thy throne." Isaiah xlv. 21: "Tell
ye, and bring them near; yea, let them take counsel together:
who hath declared this from the ancient time? have not I the
Lord? and there is no God else beside me; a just God and a
Saviour." Zephaniah iii. 5. "The just Lord is in the midst
thereof." Zechariah ix. 9: "Rejoice greatly, O daughter of Zion;
shout, O daughter of Jerusalem; behold thy King cometh unto
thee: he is just and having salvation."

8. Fourthly—Judgment. Psalm lxxxix. 14: "Justice and
judgment are the habitation of thy throne." Deuteronomy xxxii.
4: "He is the Rock, his work is perfect; for all his ways are
judgment: a God of truth and without iniquity, just and right is
he." Psalm ix. 7: "But the Lord shall endure for ever. He
hath prepared his throne for judgment." Psalm ix. 16: "The
Lord is known by the judgment which he executeth."

9. Fifthly—Mercy. Psalm lxxxix. 14: "Mercy and truth
shall go before his face." Exodus xxxiv. 6: "And the Lord
passed by before him, and proclaimed, 'The Lord, the Lord
God, merciful and gracious.' " Nehemiah ix. 17: "But thou art
a God ready to pardon, gracious and merciful."

10. And sixthly—Truth. Psalm lxxxix. 14: "Mercy and
truth shall go before thy face." Exodus xxxiv. 6: "Long-suffering and abundant in goodness and truth." Deuteronomy xxxii.
4: "He is the Rock, his work is perfect; for all his ways are
judgment: a God of truth and without iniquity, just and right is

he." Psalm xxxi. 5: "Into Thine hand I commit my spirit: thou hast redeemed me, O Lord God of Truth."

11. By a little reflection it will be seen that the idea of the existence of these attributes in the Deity is necessary to enable any rational being to exercise faith in him; for without the idea of the existence of these attributes in the Deity men could not exercise faith in him for life and salvation; seeing that without the knowledge of all things, God would not be able to save any portion of his creatures; for it is by reason of the knowledge which he has of all things, from the beginning to the end, that enables him to give that understanding to his creatures by which they are made partakers of eternal life; and if it were not for the idea existing in the minds of men that God had all knowledge it would be impossible for them to exercise faith in him.

12. And it is not less necessary that men should have the idea of the existence of the attribute power in the Deity; for unless God had power over all things, and was able by his power to control all things, and thereby deliver his creatures who put their trust in him from the power of all beings that might seek their destruction, whether in heaven, on earth, or in hell, men could not be saved. But with the idea of the existence of this attribute planted in the mind, men feel as though they had nothing to fear who put their trust in God, believing that he has power to save all who come to him to the very uttermost.

13. It is also necessary, in order to the exercise of faith in God unto life and salvation, that men should have the idea of the existence of the attribute justice in him; for without the idea of the existence of the attribute justice in the Deity, men could not have confidence sufficient to place themselves under his guidance and direction; for they would be filled with fear and doubt lest the judge of all the earth would not do right, and thus fear or doubt, existing in the mind, would preclude the possibility of the exercise of faith in him for life and salvation. But when the idea of the existence of the attribute justice in the Deity is fairly planted in the mind, it leaves no room for doubt to get into the heart, and the mind is enabled to cast itself upon the Almighty without fear and without doubt, and with the most unshaken confidence, believing that the Judge of all the earth will do right.

14. It is also of equal importance that men should have the idea of the existence of the attribute judgment in God, in order

that they may exercise faith in him for life and salvation; for without the idea of the existence of this attribute in the Deity, it would be impossible for men to exercise faith in him for life and salvation, seeing that it is through the exercise of this attribute that the faithful in Christ Jesus are delivered out of the hands of those who seek their destruction; for if God were not to come out in swift judgment against the workers of iniquity and the powers of darkness, his saints could not be saved; for it is by judgment that the Lord delivers his saints out of the hands of all their enemies, and those who reject the gospel of our Lord Jesus Christ. But no sooner is the idea of the existence of this attribute planted in the minds of men, than it gives power to the mind for the exercise of faith and confidence in God, and they are enabled by faith to lay hold on the promises which are set before them, and wade through all the tribulations and afflictions to which they are subjected by reason of the persecution from those who know not God, and obey not the gospel of our Lord Jesus Christ, believing that in due time the Lord will come out in swift judgment against their enemies, and they shall be cut off from before him, and that in his own due time he will bear them off conquerors, and more than conquerors, in all things.

15. And again, it is equally important that men should have the idea of the existence of the attribute mercy in the Deity, in order to exercise faith in him for life and salvation; for without the idea of the existence of this attribute in the Deity, the spirits of the saints would faint in the midst of the tribulations, afflictions, and persecutions which they have to endure for righteousness' sake. But when the idea of the existence of this attribute is once established in the mind it gives life and energy to the spirits of the saints, believing that the mercy of God will be poured out upon them in the midst of their afflictions, and that he will compassionate them in their sufferings, and that the mercy of God will lay hold of them and secure them in the arms of his love, so that they will receive a full reward for all their sufferings.

16. And lastly, but not less important to the exercise of faith in God, is the idea of the existence of the attribute truth in him; for without the idea of the existence of this attribute the mind of man could have nothing upon which it could rest with certainty—all would be confusion and doubt. But with the idea of the existence of this attribute in the Deity in the mind, all the

teachings, instructions, promises, and blessings, become realities, and the mind is enabled to lay hold of them with certainty and confidence, believing that these things, and all that the Lord has said, shall be fulfilled in their time; and that all the cursings, denunciations, and judgments, pronounced upon the heads of the unrighteous, will also be executed in the due time of the Lord: and, by reason of the truth and veracity of him, the mind beholds its deliverance and salvation as being certain.

17. Let the mind once reflect sincerely and candidly upon the ideas of the existence of the before-mentioned attributes in the Deity, and it will be seen that, as far as his attributes are concerned, there is a sure foundation laid for the exercise of faith in him for life and salvation. For inasmuch as God possesses the attribute knowledge, he can make all things known to his saints necessary for their salvation; and as he possesses the attribute power, he is able thereby to deliver them from the power of all enemies; and seeing, also, that justice is an attribute of the Deity, he will deal with them upon the principles of righteousness and equity, and a just reward will be granted unto them for all their afflictions and sufferings for the truth's sake. And as judgment is an attribute of the Deity also, his saints can have the most unshaken confidence that they will, in due time, obtain a perfect deliverance out of the hands of their enemies, and a complete victory over all those who have sought their hurt and destruction. And as mercy is also an attribute of the Deity, his saints can have confidence that it will be exercised towards them, and through the exercise of that attribute towards them comfort and consolation will be administered unto them abundantly, amid all their afflictions and tribulations. And, lastly, realizing that truth is an attribute of the Deity, the mind is led to rejoice amid all its trials and temptations, in hope of that glory which is to be brought at the revelation of Jesus Christ, and in view of that crown which is to be placed upon the heads of the saints in the day when the Lord shall distribute rewards unto them, and in prospect of that eternal weight of glory which the Lord has promised to bestow upon them, when he shall bring them in the midst of his throne to dwell in his presence eternally.

18. In view, then, of the existence of these attributes, the faith of the saints can become exceedingly strong, abounding in righteousness unto the praise and glory of God, and can exert its mighty influence in searching after wisdom and understanding,

until it has obtained a knowledge of all things that pertain to life and salvation.

19. Such, then, is the foundation which is laid, through the revelation of the attributes of God, for the exercise of faith in him for life and salvation; and seeing that these are attributes of the Deity, they are unchangeable—being the same yesterday, to-day, and for ever—which gives to the minds of the Latter-day Saints the same power and authority to exercise faith in God which the Former-day Saints had; so that all the saints, in this respect, have been, are, and will be, alike until the end of time; for God never changes, therefore his attributes and character remain forever the same. And as it is through the revelation of these that a foundation is laid for the exercise of faith in God unto life and salvation, the foundation, therefore, for the exercise of faith was, is, and ever will be, the same; so that all men have had, and will have, an equal privilege.

QUESTIONS AND ANSWERS ON THE FOREGOING PRINCIPLES

What was shown in the third lecture? It was shown that correct ideas of the character of God are necessary in order to exercise faith in him unto life and salvation; and that without correct ideas of his character, men could not have power to exercise faith in him unto life and salvation, but that correct ideas of his character, as far as his character was concerned in the exercise of faith in him, lay a sure foundation for the exercise of it. Lecture iv. 1.

What object had the God of Heaven in revealing his attributes to men? That through an acquaintance with his attributes they might be enabled to exercise faith in him so as to obtain eternal life. Lecture iv. 2.

Could men exercise faith in God without an acquaintance with his attributes, so as to be enabled to lay hold of eternal life? They could not. Lecture iv. 2, 3.

What account is given of the attributes of God in his revelations? First, Knowledge; secondly, Faith or Power; thirdly, Justice; fourthly, Judgment; fifthly, Mercy, and sixthly, Truth. Lecture iv. 4, 5, 6, 7, 8, 9 and 10.

Where are the revelations to be found which give this relation or the attributes of God? In the Old and New Testaments, and they are quoted in the fourth lecture, fifth, sixth, seventh, eighth, ninth and tenth paragraphs.*

*Let the student turn and commit these paragraphs to memory.

Is the idea of the existence of these attributes in the Deity
necessary in order to enable any rational being to exercise faith
in him unto life and salvation? It is.

How do you prove it? By the eleventh, twelfth, thirteenth,
fourteenth, fifteenth and sixteenth paragraphs in this lecture.*

Does the idea of the existence of these attributes in the
Deity, as far as his attributes are concerned, enable a rational
being to exercise faith in him unto life and salvation? It does.
How do you prove it? By the seventeenth and eighteenth
paragraphs.*

Have the Latter-day Saints as much authority given them,
through the revelation of the attributes of God, to exercise faith
in him as the Former-day Saints had? They have.

How do you prove it? By the nineteenth paragraph of
this lecture.*

*Let the student turn and commit these paragraphs to memory.

The Following Excerpt Is Not A Part of The Lectures On Faith

I will go back to the beginning before the world was, to show what
kind of being God is. What sort a being was God in the beginning?
Open your ears and hear, all ye ends of the earth, for I am going to
prove it to you by the Bible, and tell you the designs of God in relation
to the human race and why he interferes with the affairs of man.

*God himself was once as we are now, and is an exalted man, and sits
enthroned in yonder heavens? That is the great secret. If the vail were
rent today, and the great God who holds this world in its orbit, and who
upholds all worlds and all things by his power, was to make himself visible*

*I say, if you were to see him today, you would see him like a man in
form—like yourselves in all the person, image, and very form as a man;
for Adam was created in the very fashion, image and likeness of God, and
received instruction from, and walked, talked, and conversed with him,
as one man talks and communes with another.* * * * I wish I was in a
suitable place to tell it, and that I had the trumpet of an archangel, so that
I could tell the story in such a manner that persecution would cease
forever. What did Jesus say? (Mark it, Elder Rigdon!) The scriptures inform us that Jesus said, As the Father hath power to himself,
even so hath the Son power—to do what? Why, what the Father did.
The answer is obvious—in a manner to lay down his body and take
it up again. Jesus, what are you going to do? To lay down my life
as my Father did, and take it up again. Do you believe it? If you do
not believe it, you do not believe the Bible. The scriptures say it and
I defy all the learning and wisdom and all the combined powers of earth
and hell together to refute it. "King Follett" discourse, by Joseph the
Prophet. See *The Vision*, pp. 17-18.

LECTURE FIFTH.

1. In our former lectures we treated of the being, character, perfections, and attributes, of God. What we mean by perfections is, the perfections which belong to all the attributes of his nature. We shall, in this lecture, speak of the Godhead—we mean the Father, Son, and Holy Spirit.

2. There are two personages who constitute the great, matchless, governing, and supreme power over all things, by whom all things were created and made, that are created and made, whether visible or invisible, whether in heaven, on earth, or in the earth, under the earth, or throughout the immensity of space. They are the Father and the Son—the Father being a personage of spirit, glory, and power, possessing all perfection and fullness, the Son, who was in the bosom of the Father, a personage of tabernacle, made or fashioned like unto man, or being in the form and likeness of man, or rather man was formed after his likeness and in his image; he is also the express image and likeness of the personage of the Father, possessing all the fullness of the Father, or the same fullness with the Father; being begotten of him, and ordained from before the foundation of the world to be a propitiation for the sins of all those who should believe on his name, and is called the Son because of the flesh, and descended in suffering below that which man can suffer; or, in other words, suffered greater sufferings, and was exposed to more powerful contradictions than any man can be. But, notwithstanding all this, he kept the law of God, and remained without sin, showing thereby that it is in the power of man to keep the law and remain also without sin; and also, that by him a righteous judgment might come upon all flesh, and that all who walk not in the law of God may justly be condemned by the law, and have no excuse for their sins. And he being the Only-Begotten of the Father, full of grace and truth, and having overcome, received a fullness of the glory of the Father, possessing the same mind with the Father, which mind is the Holy Spirit, that bears record of the Father and the Son, and these three are one; or, in other words, these three constitute the great, matchless, governing and supreme power over all things; by whom all things were created and made that were created and made, and these three constitute the Godhead, and are one; the Father and

the Son possessing the same mind, the same wisdom, glory, power, and fullness—filling all in all; the Son being filled with the fullness of the mind, glory, and power; or, in other words, the spirit, glory, and power, of the Father, possessing all knowledge and glory, and the same kingdom, sitting at the right hand of power, in the express image and likeness of the Father, mediator for man, being filled with the fullness of the mind of the Father; or, in other words, the Spirit of the Father, which Spirit is shed forth upon all who believe on his name and keep his commandments; and all those who keep his commandments shall grow up from grace to grace, and become heirs of the heavenly kingdom, and joint heirs with Jesus Christ; possessing the same mind, being transformed into the same image or likeness, even the express image of him who fills all in all; being filled with the fullness of his glory, and become one in him, even as the Father, Son and Holy Spirit are one.

3. From the foregoing account of the Godhead, which is given in his revelations, the saints have a sure foundation laid for the exercise of faith unto life and salvation, through the atonement and mediation of Jesus Christ; by whose blood they have a forgiveness of sins, and also a sure reward laid up for them in heaven, even that of partaking of the fullness of the Father and the Son through the Spirit. As the Son partakes of the fullness of the Father through the Spirit, so the saints are, by the same Spirit, to be partakers of the same fullness, to enjoy the same glory; for as the Father and the Son are one, so, in like manner, the saints are to be one in them. Through the love of the Father, the mediation of Jesus Christ, and the gift of the Holy Spirit, they are to be heirs of God, and joint heirs with Jesus Christ. (See footnote at end of Lecture 5.)

QUESTIONS AND ANSWERS ON THE FOREGOING PRINCIPLES

Of what do the foregoing lectures treat? Of the being, perfections, and attributes of the Deity. Lecture v. 1.

What are we to understand by the perfections of the Deity? The perfections which belong to his attributes.

How many personages are there in the Godhead? Two: the Father and Son. Lecture v. 1. (See footnote.)

How do you prove that there are two personages in the Godhead? By the Scriptures. Genesis i. 26. Also lecture ii. 6: "As the Lord God said unto the Only Begotten, who was with him from the beginning, 'Let us make man in our image, after our likeness'—and it was done." Genesis iii. 22: "And the Lord God said unto the Only Begotten, 'Behold, the man is become as one of us: to know good and evil.'" John xvii. 5: "And now, O Father, glorify thou me with thine own self with the glory which I had with thee before the world was." Lecture v. 2.

What is the Father? He is a personage of glory and of power. Lecture v. 2.

How do you prove that the Father is a personage of glory and of power? Isaiah lx. 19: "The sun shall be no more thy light by day, neither for brightness shall the moon give light unto thee; but the Lord shall be unto thee an everlasting light, and thy God thy glory." 1 Chronicles xxix. 11: "Thine, O Lord, is the greatness, and the power, and the glory." Psalm xxix. 3: "The voice of the Lord is upon the waters: the God of glory thunders." Psalm lxxix. 9: "Help us, O God of our salvation, for the glory of thy name." Romans i. 23: "And changed the glory of the incorruptible God into an image made like to corruptible man." Secondly, of power. 1 Chronicles xxix. 11: "Thine, O Lord, is the greatness, and the power, and glory." Jeremiah xxxii. 17: "Ah! Lord God, behold thou hast made the earth and the heavens by thy great power, and stretched-out arm; and there is nothing too hard for thee." Deuteronomy iv. 37: "And because he loved thy fathers, therefore he chose their seed after them, and brought them out in his sight with his mighty power." 2 Samuel xxii. 33: "God is my strength and power." Job xxvi., commencing with the 7th verse to the end of the chapter: "He stretcheth out the north over the empty place, and hangeth the earth upon nothing. He bindeth up the waters in his thick clouds; and the cloud is not rent under them. He holdeth back the face of his throne, and spreadeth his cloud upon it. He hath compassed the waters with bounds, until the day and night come to an end. The pillars of heaven tremble, and are astonished at his reproof. He divideth the sea with his power, and by his understanding he smiteth through the proud. By his Spirit he hath garnished the heavens; his hand hath formed the crooked serpent. Lo, these are parts of his ways! but how little a portion is heard of him? But the thunder of his power who can understand?"

What is the Son? First, he is a personage of tabernacle. Lecture v. 2.

How do you prove it? John xiv. 9, 10, 11: "Jesus saith unto him, 'Have I been so long time with you, and yet hast thou not known me, Philip? He that hath seen me hath seen the Father; and how sayest thou then, Show us the Father? Believest thou not that I am in the Father, and the Father in me? The words that I speak unto you I speak not of myself: but the Father that dwelleth in me he doeth the works. Believe me that I am in the Father and the Father in me.'" Secondly,—and being a personage of tabernacle, was made or fashioned like unto man, or being in the form and likeness of man. Lecture v. 2. Philippians ii. 2-8: "Let this mind be in you, which was also in Christ Jesus; who, being in the form of God, thought it not robbery to be equal with God; but made himself of no reputation, and took upon him the form of a servant, and was made in the likeness of man, and being found in fashion as a man, he humbled himself, and became obedient unto death, even the death of the cross." Hebrews ii. 14, 16: "Forasmuch then as the children are partakers of flesh and blood, he also himself likewise took part of the same. For verily he took not on him the nature of angels: but he took on him the seed of Abraham." Thirdly, he is also in the likeness of the personage of the Father. Lecture v. 2. Hebrews i. 1, 2, 3: "God, who at sundry times and in divers manners, spake in times past to the fathers, by the prophets, hath in these last days spoken unto us by his Son, whom he hath appointed heir of all things, by whom also he made the worlds, who being the brightness of his glory, and the express image of his person." Again, Philippians ii. 5, 6: "Let this mind be in you, which was also in Christ Jesus; who, being in the form of God, thought it not robbery to be equal with God."

Was it by the Father and the Son that all things were created and made that were created and made? It was. Colossians i. 15, 16, 17: "Who is the image of the invisible God, the first born of every creature; for by him were all things created that are in heaven and that are in earth, visible and invisible, whether they be thrones or dominions, principalities or powers; all things were created by him and for him; and he is before all things, and by him all things consist." Genesis i. 1: "In the beginning God created the heavens and the earth." Hebrews i. 2: (God) "Hath in these last days spoken unto us by his Son, whom he hath appointed heir of all things, by whom also he made the worlds."

Does he possess the fullness of the Father? He does.

Colossians i. 19, ii. 9: "For it pleased the Father that in him should all fullness dwell." "For in him dwelleth all the fullness of the Godhead bodily." Ephesians i. 23: "Which is his (Christ's) body, the fullness of him that fills all in all."

Why was he called the Son? Because of the flesh. Luke i. 33: "That holy thing which shall be born of thee, shall be called the Son of God." Matthew iii. 16, 17: "And Jesus, when he was baptized, went up straightway out of the water, and lo, the heavens were opened unto him, and he (John) saw the Spirit of God descending like a dove and lighting upon him: and lo, a voice from heaven saying, 'This is my beloved Son, in whom I am well pleased.'"

Was he ordained of the Father, from before the foundation of the world, to be a propitiation for the sins of all those who should believe on his name? He was. 1 Peter i. 18, 19, 20: "Forasmuch as ye know that ye were not redeemed with corruptible things, as silver and gold, from your vain conversation, received by tradition from your fathers: but with the precious blood of Christ, as of a lamb without blemish and without spot; who verily was foreordained before the foundation of the world, but was manifested in these last times for you." Revelations xiii. 8: "And all that dwell upon the earth shall worship him (the beast), whose names are not written in the book of life of the Lamb slain from the foundation of the world." 1 Corinthians ii. 7: "But we speak the wisdom of God in a mystery, even the hidden mystery, which God ordained before the world, unto our glory."

Do the Father and the Son possess the same mind? They do. John v. 30: "I (Christ) can of my own self do nothing: as I hear, I judge, and my judgment is just; because I seek not my own will, but the will of the Father who sent me." John vi. 38: "For I (Christ) came down from heaven, not to do my own will, but the will of him that sent me." John x. 30: "I (Christ) and my Father are one."

What is this mind? The Holy Spirit. John xv. 26: "But when the Comforter is come, whom I will send unto you from the Father, even the Spirit of truth, which proceeds from the Father, he shall testify of me (Christ)." Galatians iv. 6: "And because ye are sons, God hath sent forth the Spirit of his Son into your hearts."

Do the Father, Son, and Holy Spirit constitute the God-head? They do. Lecture v. 2.* (See footnote.)

Do the believers in Christ Jesus, through the gift of the Spirit, become one with the Father and the Son, as the Father and the Son are one? They do. John xvii. 20, 21: "Neither pray I for these (the apostles) alone, but for them also who shall believe on me through their word; that they all may be one; as thou, Father, art in me, and I in thee, that they also may be one in us, that the world may believe that thou hast sent me."

Does the foregoing account of the Godhead lay a sure foundation for the exercise of faith in him unto life and salvation? It does.

How do you prove it? By the third paragraph of this lecture.*

*Let the student commit these paragraphs to memory.

(Note:—That which follows has been added only in this compilation and, of course, is no part of the Lectures on Faith as originally delivered in Kirtland.) Further light was revealed to the Prophet subsequent to the giving of these Lectures, as will be noted by the quotations following—

A. We believe in God the Eternal Father, and in His Son Jesus Christ, and in the Holy Ghost. — Joseph Smith (See famous Wentworth letter, March 1, 1842, Documentary History of the Church, Vol. 4:540)

B. The Father has a body of flesh and bones as tangible as man's; the Son also; but the Holy Ghost has not a body of flesh and bones, but is a personage of Spirit. Were it not so, the Holy Ghost could not dwell in us. April 2,1843, Doc. and Cov., Sec. 130:22.

The Holy Ghost and the Holy Spirit

By Pres. Joseph F. Smith

But the gift of the Holy Ghost, which bears record of the Father and the Son, which takes of the things of the Father and shows them unto man, which testifies of Jesus Christ, and of the ever-living God, the Father of Jesus Christ, and which bears witness of the truth-this Spirit, this intelligence is not given unto all men until they repent of their sins and come into a state of worthiness before the Lord. Then they receive it by the laying on of the hands of those who are authorized of God to bestow His blessings upon the heads of the children of men. The Spirit spoken of in that which I have read is that Spirit which will not cease to strive with the children of men until they are brought to the possession of the greater light and intelligence. Though a man may commit all manner of sin and blasphemy, if he has not received the testimony of the Holy Ghost he may be forgiven by repenting of his sins, humbling himself before the Lord, and obeying in sincerity the commandments of God. As it is stated here: "Every soul who forsaketh his sins and cometh unto me, and calleth on my name, and obeyeth my voice, and keepeth my commandments, shall see my face and know that I am." He shall be forgiven and receive the greater light: he will enter into a solemn covenant with God, into a compact with the Almighty, through the Only Begotten Son, whereby he becomes a son of God, an heir of God, and a joint heir with Jesus Christ. Then if he shall sin against the light and knowledge he has received, the light that was within him shall become darkness, and oh, how great will be that darkness! Then, and not till then, will this Spirit of Christ that lighteth every man that cometh into the world cease to strive with him, and he shall be left to his own destruction.

This is in accordance with the doctrine of Christ, as it is revealed in the New Testament; it is in accordance with the word of God as it is revealed in the latter-day through the Prophet Joseph Smith. God will not condemn any man to utter destruction, neither shall any man be thrust down to hell irredeemably, until he has been brought to the possession of the greater light that comes through repentance and obedience to the laws and commandments of God; but if, after he has received light and knowledge, he shall sin against the light and will not repent, then, indeed, he becomes a lost soul, a son of perdition.

The question is often asked, is there any difference between the Spirit of the Lord and the Holy Ghost? The terms are frequently used synonymously. We often say the Spirit of God when we mean the Holy Ghost; we likewise say the Holy Ghost when we mean the Spirit of God. The Holy Ghost is a personage in the Godhead, and is not that which lighteth every man that comes into the world. It is the Spirit of God which proceeds through Christ to the world, that enlightens every man that comes into the world, and that strives with the children of men, and will continue to strive with them, until it brings them to a knowledge of the truth and the possession of the greater light and testimony of the Holy Ghost. If, however, he receive that greater light, and then sin against it, the Spirit of God will cease to strive with him, and the Holy Ghost will wholly depart from him. Then will he persecute the truth; then will he seek the blood of the innocent; then will he not scruple at the commission of any crime; except so far as he may fear the penalties of the law, in consequence of the crime, upon himself.

Improvement Era, Vol. 11:380-2

In order that additional information may be available on the Godhead and the Holy Ghost, the following references are listed:—

The Holy Ghost:

Contributor: 2:70; 3:7; 4:256; -259; 6:301; 6:303; 6:410; 15:13.

Improvement Era: 1:760; 3:116; 5:35; 5:474; 11:380-1-2; 6:629; 12:393; 12:409; 12:389; 16:11; 17:706; 19:460; 20:39; 20:71; 26:1149; 28:168.

Times and Seasons: 2:430; 3:752; 3:823; 3:866; 3:890; 3:904; 3:915; 3:955; 3:945; 4:23; 6:768.

Journals of Discourses: 1:24; 1:50; 1:90; 1:240; 2:231; 3:183; 3:203; 4:20; 4:140; 4:189; 4:266; 5:179; 5:203; 6:5; 6:105; 6:95; 6:349; 7:118; 7:178; 7:266; 8:102; 8:44; 9:254; 12:34; 12:112.

Liahona: 5:297; 5:354; 5:550; 5:1031; 5:1139; 5:1269; 6:176; 6:175; 6:482; 6:792; 6:957; 6:986; 7:203; 7:314; 7:668; 8:625-6; 9:711-2; 9:273; 9:691; 9:673; 9:689; 10:312; 10:564; 10:656; 11:178; 11:205; 11:191; 11:848; 12:670; 12:759; 13:51; 13:52; 13:35; 13:386; 13:597; 16:1195; 18:35; 18·482; 18:484; 20:1; 20:5; 21:300; 21:379.

Documentary History of Church: 1:61.78; 1:163; 2:477; 3:379-80; 4:555; 5:26; 6:261; 5:555; 6:58; 6:253.

The Godhead

Improvement Era: 4:463; 20:34; 23:97; 17:706; 1:754; 23:496; 2:894; 2:833; 4:228; 17:706; 25:579.

Liahona: 19:442; 20:442; 12:648; 7:41; 8:673; 7:41-42; 7:109.

D. H. C.: 5:426.

Contributor: 4:214.

J. D.: 6.1; 4:215,271; 5:331; 6:275; 6:95. 1:238; 12:68-9; 11:40-2; 11:119-24; 11:268; 11:271; 26:18.

Journal History, Feb. 18, 1855, pp. 1-2.

Millennial Star, 9:135.

For a masterful presentation of the Doctrines of the Holy Trinity and the Atonement, consult the Third, Fourth and Fifth Year Books of the Seventy's Course in Theology, written by Pres. B. H. Roberts, and entitled: The Doctrine of Deity, (3rd), The Atonement (4th), and Divine Immanence and the Holy Ghost, (5th). Also refer to: *The Mormon Doctrine of Deity*, this being the Roberts — Vander Donkt discussion on the Godhead. These represent the epitome of instruction on these important subjects. Nothing further need be said after reading these masterpieces.

The true God exists both in time and in space, and has as much relation to them as man or any other being. He has extension, and form, and dimensions, as well as man. He occupies space; has a body, parts and passions; can go from place to place—can eat, drink, and talk, as well as man. Man resembles Him in the features and form of His body, and He does not differ materially in size. When He has been seen among men, He has been pronounced, even by the wicked, as one of their own species. So much did He look like man, that some supposed Him to be the carpenter's son. Like man, He had a Father; and He was the "express image of the person of the Father." The two persons were as much alike in form, in size, and in every other respect as fathers and sons are of the human race; indeed, the human race are "His off-spring," made in His likeness and image, not after His moral image, but after the image of His person. There is no such thing as moral image. Such an image cannot exist. Morality is a property of some being or substance. A property without a substance or being to which it appertains is inconceivable. A property can never have figure, shape, or image of any kind. Hence, a moral image never had an existence except in the brains of modern idolators.—By Orson Pratt. *The Kingdom of God*, No. 2, p. 4, Liverpool, October 31, 1848.

LECTURE SIXTH

1. Having treated in the preceding lectures of the ideas, of the character, perfections, and attributes of God, we next proceed to treat of the knowledge which persons must have, that the course of life which they pursue is according to the will of God, in order that they may be enabled to exercise faith in him unto life and salvation.

2. This knowledge supplies an important place in revealed religion; for it was by reason of it that the ancients were enabled to endure as seeing him who is invisible. An actual knowledge to any person, that the course of life which he pursues is according to the will of God, is essentially necessary to enable him to have that confidence in God without which no person can obtain eternal life. It was this that enabled the ancient saints to endure all their afflictions and persecutions, and to take joyfully the spoiling of their goods, knowing (not believing merely) that they had a more enduring substance. Hebrews x. 34.

3. Having the assurance that they were pursuing a course which was agreeable to the will of God, they were enabled to take, not only the spoiling of their goods, and the wasting of their substance, joyfully, but also to suffer death in its most horrid forms; knowing (not merely believing) that when this earthly house of their tabernacle was dissolved, they had a building of God, a house not made with hands, eternal in the heavens. 2 Corinthians v. 1.

4. Such was, and always will be, the situation of the saints of God, that unless they have an actual knowledge that the course they are pursuing is according to the will of God they will grow weary in their minds, and faint; for such has been, and always will be, the opposition in the hearts of unbelievers and those that know not God against the pure and unadulterated religion of heaven (the only thing which insures eternal life), that they will persecute to the uttermost all that worship God according to his revelations, receive the truth in the love of it, and submit themselves to be guided and directed by his will; and drive them to such extremities that nothing short of an actual knowledge of their being the favorites of heaven, and of their having embraced the order of things which God has established for the redemption of man, will enable them to exercise that confidence in him,

necessary for them to overcome the world, and obtain that crown of glory which is laid up for them that fear God.

5. For a man to lay down his all, his character and reputation, his honor, and applause, his good name among men, his houses, his lands, his brothers and sisters, his wife and children, and even his own life also—counting all things but filth and dross for the excellency of the knowledge of Jesus Christ— requires more than mere belief or supposition that he is doing the will of God; but actual knowledge, realizing that, when these sufferings are ended, he will enter into eternal rest, and be a partaker of the glory of God.

6. For unless a person does know that he is walking according to the will of God, it would be offering an insult to the dignity of the Creator were he to say that he would be a partaker of his glory when he should be done with the things of this life. But when he has this knowledge, and most assuredly knows that he is doing the will of God, his confidence can be equally strong that he will be a partaker of the glory of God.

7. Let us here observe, that a religion that does not require the sacrifice of all things never has power sufficient to produce the faith necessary unto life and salvation; for, from the first existence of man, the faith necessary unto the enjoyment of life and salvation never could be obtained without the sacrifice of all earthly things. It was through this sacrifice, and this only, that God has ordained that men should enjoy eternal life; and it is through the medium of the sacrifice of all earthly things that men do actually know that they are doing the things that are well pleasing in the sight of God. When a man has offered in sacrifice all that he has for the truth's sake, not even withholding his life, and believing before God that he has been called to make this sacrifice because he seeks to do his will, he does know, most assuredly, that God does and will accept his sacrifice and offering, and that he has not, nor will not seek his face in vain. Under these circumstances, then, he can obtain the faith necessary for him to lay hold on eternal life.

8. It is in vain for persons to fancy to themselves that they are heirs with those, or can be heirs with them, who have offered their all in sacrifice, and by this means obtain faith in God and favor with him so as to obtain eternal life, unless they, in like manner, offer unto him the same sacrifice, and through that offering obtain the knowledge that they are accepted of him.

9. It was in offering sacrifices that Abel, the first martyr, obtained knowledge that he was accepted of God. And from the days of righteous Abel to the present time, the knowledge that men have that they are accepted in the sight of God is obtained by offering sacrifice. And in the last days, before the Lord comes, he is to gather together his saints who have made a covenant with him by sacrifice. Psalm 1: 3, 4, 5: "Our God shall come, and shall not keep silence: a fire shall devour before him, and it shall be very tempestuous round about him. He shall call to the heavens from above, and to the earth, that he may judge his people. Gather my saints together unto me; those that have made a covenant with me by sacrifice."

10. Those, then, who make the sacrifice, will have the testimony that their course is pleasing in the sight of God; and those who have this testimony will have faith to lay hold on eternal life, and will be enabled, through faith, to endure unto the end, and receive the crown that is laid up for them that love the appearing of our Lord Jesus Christ. But those who do not make the sacrifice cannot enjoy this faith, because men are dependent upon this sacrifice in order to obtain this faith: therefore, they cannot lay hold upon eternal life, because the revelations of God do not guarantee unto them the authority so to do, and without this guarantee faith could not exist.

11. All the saints of whom we have account, in all the revelations of God which are extant, obtained the knowledge which they had of their acceptance in his sight through the sacrifice which they offered unto him; and through the knowledge thus obtained their faith became sufficiently strong to lay hold upon the promise of eternal life, and to endure as seeing him who is invisible; and were enabled, through faith, to combat the powers of darkness, contend against the wiles of the adversary, overcome the world, and obtain the end of their faith, even the salvation of their souls.

12. But those who have not made this sacrifice to God do not know that the course which they pursue is well pleasing in his sight; for whatever may be their belief or their opinion, it is a matter of doubt and uncertainty in their mind; and where doubt and uncertainty are there faith is not, nor can it be. For doubt and faith do not exist in the same person at the same time; so that persons whose minds are under doubts and fears cannot have unshaken confidence; and where unshaken confidence is

not there faith is weak; and where faith is weak the persons will
not be able to contend against all the opposition, tribulations, and
afflictions which they will have to encounter in order to be heirs
of God, and joint heirs with Christ Jesus; and they will grow
weary in their minds, and the adversary will have power over
them and destroy them.

This Lecture is so plain, and the facts set forth so self-evident that
it is deemed unnecessary to form a catechism upon it: the student is, therefore, instructed to commit the whole to memory.

The Following Excerpt Is Not A Part of The Lectures On Faith

There have been various species of idolatry in different ages of the
world. The sun, moon, stars, beasts, crocodiles, frightful serpents, images
of wood, of stone, and of brass, have been erected into gods, and wor-
shipped by innumerable multitudes. But the system of idolatry, invented
by modern christianity, far surpasses in absurdity anything that we have
ever heard of. One of the celebrated worshippers of this newly-discovered
god, in his *Physical Theory of Another Life,* says, "A disembodied spirit,
or, we would rather say, an unembodied spirit, or sheer mind, is
NOWHERE. Place is a relation belonging to extension; and extension
is a property of matter; but that which is wholly abstracted from matter,
and in speaking of which we deny that it has any property in common
therewith, can in itself be subject to none of its conditions; and we
might as well say of a pure spirit that it is hard, heavy, or red, or that
it is a cubic foot in dimensions, as say that it is *here or there.* It is
only in a popular and improper sense that any such affirmation is made
concerning the Infinite Spirit, or that we speak of God as everywhere
present. God is in every place in a sense, altogether incomprehensible
by finite minds, inasmuch as his relation to space and extension is
peculiar to infinitude. Using the terms as we use them of ourselves,
God is not HERE OR THERE, any more than he exists NOW AND
THEN." This species of idolatry, according to the foregoing quotation,
approaches so near to Atheism, that no one can tell the difference. Reader,
can you see the difference? A god "without a body!" A god "without
parts!" A god that cannot be "here or there!" A god that is "nowhere!" A god that canont exist "now and then!" A god that exists
in NO TIME. A god that has no extension—no "parts"—no con-

(*Continued on page* 69)

LECTURE SEVENTH.

1. In preceding lessons we treated of what faith was, and of the object on which it rested. Agreeable to our plan, we now proceed to speak of its effects.

2. As we have seen in our former lectures that faith was the principle of action and of power in all intelligent beings, both in heaven and on earth, it will not be expected that we shall, in a lecture of this description, attempt to unfold all its effects; neither is it necessary to our purpose so to do, for it would embrace all things in heaven and on earth, and encompass all the creations of God, with all their endless varieties; for no world has yet been framed that was not framed by faith, neither has there been an intelligent being on any of God's creations who did not get there by reason of faith as it existed in himself or in some other being; nor has there been a change or a revolution in any of the creations of God, but it has been effected by faith; neither will there be a change or a revolution, unless it is effected in the same way, in any of the vast creations of the Almighty, for it is by faith that the Deity works.

3. Let us here offer some explanation in relation to faith, that our meaning may be clearly comprehended. We ask, then, what are we to understand by a man's working by faith? We answer—we understand that when a man works by faith he works by mental exertion instead of physical force. It is by words, instead of exerting his physical powers, with which every being works when he works by faith. God said, "Let there be light, and there was light." Joshua spake, and the great lights whcih God had created stood still. Elijah commanded, and the heavens were stayed for the space of three years and six months, so that it did not rain: he again commanded and the heavens gave forth rain. All this was done by faith. And the Savior says, "If you have faith as a grain of mustard seed, say to this mountain, 'Remove,' and it will remove; or say to that sycamine tree, 'Be ye plucked up, and planted in the midst of the sea,' and it shall obey you." Faith, then, works by words; and with these its mightiest works have been, and will be, performed.

4. It surely will not be required of us to prove that this is the principle upon which all eternity has acted and will act; for every reflecting mind must know that it is by reason of this power

that all the hosts of heaven perform their works of wonder, majesty, and glory. Angels move from place to place by virtue of this power; it is by reason of it that they are enabled to descend from heaven to earth; and were it not for the power of faith they never could be ministering spirits to them who should be heirs of salvation, neither could they act as heavenly messengers, for they would be destitute of the power necessary to enable them to do the will of God.

5. It is only necessary for us to say that the whole visible creation, as it now exists, is the effect of faith. It was faith by which it was framed, and it is by the power of faith that it continues in its organized form, and by which the planets move round their orbits and sparkle forth their glory. So, then, faith is truly the first principle in the science of THEOLOGY, and, when understood, leads the mind back to the beginning, and carries it forward to the end; or, in other words, from eternity to eternity.

6. As faith, then, is the principle by which the heavenly hosts perform their works, and by which they enjoy all their felicity, we might expect to find it set forth in a revelation from God as the principle upon which his creatures here below must act in order to obtain the felicities enjoyed by the saints in the eternal world; and that, when God would undertake to raise up men for the enjoyment of himself, he would teach them the necessity of living by faith, and the impossibility there was of their enjoying the blessedness of eternity without it, seeing that all the blessings of eternity are the effects of faith.

7. Therefore it is said, and appropriately too, that "Without faith it is impossible to please God." If it should be asked— Why is it impossible to please God without faith? The answer would be—Because without faith it is impossible for men to be saved; and as God desires the salvation of men, he must, of course, desire that they should have faith; and he could not be pleased unless they had, or else he could be pleased with their destruction.

8. From this we learn that the many exhortations which have been given by inspired men, to those who had received the word of the Lord to have faith in him, were not mere commonplace matters, but were for the best of all reasons, and that was— because without it there was no salvation, neither in this world nor in that which is to come. When men begin to live by faith they begin to draw near to God; and when faith is perfected they

are like him; and because he is saved they are saved also; for they will be in the same situation he is in, because they have come to him; and when he appears they shall be like him, for they will see him as he is.

9. As all the visible creation is an effect of faith, so is salvation also—we mean salvation in its most extensive latitude of interpretation, whether it is temporal or spiritual. In order to have this subject clearly set before the mind, let us ask what situation must a person be in in order to be saved? or what is the difference between a saved man and one who is not saved? We answer, from what we have before seen of the heavenly worlds, they must be persons who can work by faith and who are able, by faith, to be ministering spirits to them who shall be heirs of salvation; and they must have faith to enable them to act in the presence of the Lord, otherwise they cannot be saved. And what constitutes the real difference between a saved person and one not saved is—the difference in the degree of their faith —one's faith has become perfect enough to lay hold upon eternal life, and the other's has not. But to be a little more particular, let us ask—Where shall we find a prototype into whose likeness we may be assimilated, in order that we may be made partakers of life and salvation? or, in other words, where shall we find a saved being? for if we can find a saved being, we may ascertain without much difficulty what all others must be in order to be saved. We think that it will not be a matter of dispute, that two beings who are unlike each other cannot both be saved; for whatever constitutes the salvation of one will constitute the salvation of every creature which will be saved; and if we find one saved being in all existence, we may see what all others must be, or else not be saved. We ask, then, where is the prototype? or where is the saved being? We conclude, as to the answer of this question, there will be no dispute among those who believe the Bible, that it is Christ: all will agree in this, that he is the prototype or standard of salvation; or, in other words, that he is a saved being. And if we should continue our interrogation, and ask how it is that he is saved? the answer would be—because he is a just and holy being; and if he were anything different from what he is, he would not be saved; for his salvation depends on his being precisely what he is and nothing else; for if it were possible for him to change, in the least degree, so sure he would fail of salvation and lose all his dominion, power, authority and

glory, which constitute salvation; for salvation consists in the glory, authority, majesty, power and dominion which Jehovah possesses and in nothing else; and no being can possess it but himself or one like him. Thus says John, in his first epistle, third chapter, second and third verses: "Beloved, now are we the sons of God, and it doth not yet appear what we shall be; but we know that, when he shall appear, we shall be like him, for we shall see him as he is. And every man that hath this hope in him, purifieth himself, even as he is pure." Why purify themselves as he is pure? Because if they do not they cannot be like him.

10. The Lord said unto Moses, Leviticus xix. 2: "Speak unto all the congregation of the children of Israel, and say unto them, 'Ye shall be holy: for I the Lord your God am holy.'" And Peter says, first epistle, i. 15, 16: "But as he which hath called you is holy, so be ye holy in all manner of conversation; because it is written, 'Be ye holy; for I am holy.'" And the Saviour says, Matthew v. 48: "Be ye therefore perfect, even as your Father which is in heaven is perfect.'" If any should ask, why all these sayings? the answer is to be found from what is before quoted from John's epistle, that when he (the Lord) shall appear, the saints will be like him; and if they are not holy, as he is holy, and perfect, as he is perfect, they cannot be like him; for no being can enjoy his glory without possessing his perfections and holiness, no more than they could reign in his kingdom without his power.

11. This clearly sets forth the propriety of the Saviour's saying, recorded in John's testimony, xiv. 12: "Verily, verily, I say unto you, he that believeth on me, the works that I do shall he do also; and greater works than these shall he do, because I go unto my Father." This taken in connection with some of the sayings in the Savior's prayer, recorded in the seventeenth chapter, gives great clearness to his expressions. He says in the 20, 21, 22, 23, and 24th verses: "Neither pray I for these alone, but for them also who shall believe on me through their words; that they all may be one; as thou, Father, art in me, and I in thee, that they also may be one in us; that the world may believe that thou hast sent me. And the glory which thou gavest me I have given them; that they may be one, even as we are one: I in them, and thou in me, that they may be made perfect in one; and that the world may know that thou hast sent me,

and hast loved them, as thou has loved me. Father, I will
that they also whom thou has given me, be with me where I
am; that they may behold my glory, which thou hast given
me: for thou lovedst me before the foundation of the world."

12. All these sayings put together give as clear an account
of the state of the glorified saints as language could give—the
works that Jesus had done they were to do, and greater works
than those which he had done among them should they do, and
that because he went to the Father. He does not say that they
should do these works in time; but they should do greater works,
because he went to the Father. He says in the 24th verse:
"Father, I will that they also, whom thou hast given me, be with
me where I am; that they may behold my glory." These sayings,
taken in connection, make it very plain that the greater works
which those that believed on his name were to do were to be done
in eternity, where he was going and where they should behold his
glory. He had said, in another part of his prayer, that he desired
of his Father that those who believed on him should be one in
him, as he and the Father were one in each other. "Neither pray
I for these (the apostles) alone, but for them also who shall
believe on me through their words, that they all may be one";
that is, they who believe on him through the apostles' words, as
well as the apostles themselves, "that they all may be one, as
thou, Father, are in me and I in thee; that they also may be one
in us."

13. What language can be plainer than this? The Saviour
surely intended to be understood by his disciples, and he so spake
that they might understand him; for he declares to his Father,
in language, not to be easily mistaken, that he wanted his disciples,
even all of them, to be as himself and the Father, for as he and
the Father were one so they might be one with them. And
what is said in the 22nd verse is calculated to more firmly establish this belief; if it needs anything to establish it. He says:
"And the glory which thou gavest me, I have given them, that
they may be one, even as we are one." As much as to say that
unless they have the glory which the Father had given him they
could not be one with them; for he says he had given them the
glory that the Father had given him that they might be one; or
in other words, to make them one.

14. This fills up the measure of information on this subject,
and shows most clearly that the Saviour wished his disciples to

understand that they were to be partakers with him in all things, not even his glory excepted.

15. It is scarcely necessary here to observe what we have previously noticed, that the glory which the Father and the Son have is because they are just and holy beings; and that if they were lacking in one attribute or perfection which they have, the glory which they have never could be enjoyed by them, for it requires them to be precisely what they are in order to enjoy it; and if the Saviour gives this glory to any others, he must do it in the very way set forth in his prayer to his Father—by making them one with him as he and the Father are one. In so doing he would give them the glory which the Father has given him; and when his disciples are made one with the Father and Son, as the Father and Son are one, who cannot see the propriety of the Saviour's saying—"The works which I do, shall they do; and greater works than these shall they do, because I go to my Father."

16. These teachings of the Saviour most clearly show unto us the nature of salvation, and what he proposed unto the human family when he proposed to save them—that he proposed to make them like unto himself, and he was like the Father, the great prototype of all saved beings; and for any portion of the human family to be assimilated into their likeness is to be saved; and to be unlike them is to be destroyed; and on this hinge turns the door of salvation.

17. Who cannot see, then, that salvation is the effect of faith? for, as we have previously observed, all the heavenly beings work by this principle; and it is because they are able so to do that they are saved, for nothing but this could save them. And this is the lesson which the God of heaven, by the mouth of his holy prophets, has been endeavoring to teach to the world. Hence we are told, that "Without faith it is impossible to please God"; and that salvation is of faith, that it might be by grace, to the end the promise might be sure to all the seed. Romans iv. 16. And that Israel, who followed after the law of righteousness, has not attained to the law of righteousness. Wherefore? Because they sought it not by faith, but as it were by the works of the law; for they stumbled at that stumbling stone. Romans ix. 32. And Jesus said unto the man who brought his son to him, to get the devil who tormented him cast out: "If thou canst believe, all things are possible to him that believeth."

Mark ix. 23. These with a multitude of other scriptures which might be quoted plainly set forth the light in which the Saviour, as well as the Former-day Saints, viewed the plan of salvation. That it was a system of faith—it begins with faith, and continues by faith; and every blessing which is obtained in relation to it is the effect of faith, whether it pertains to this life or that which is to come. To this all the revelations of God bear witness. If there were children of promise, they were the effects of faith, not even the Saviour of the world excepted. "Blessed is she that believed," said Elizabeth to Mary, when she went to visit her, "for there shall be a performance of those things which were told her from the Lord." Luke i. 45. Nor was the birth of John the Baptist the less a matter of faith; for in order that his father Zacharias might believe he was struck dumb. And through the whole history of the scheme of life and salvation, it is a matter of faith: every man received according to his faith—according as his faith was, so were his blessings and privileges; and nothing was withheld from him when his faith was sufficient to receive it. He could stop the mouths of lions, quench the violence of fire, escape the edge of the sword, wax valiant in fight, and put to flight the armies of the aliens; women could, by their faith, receive their dead children to life again; in a word, there was nothing impossible with them who had faith. All things were in subjection to the Former-day Saints, according as their faith was. By their faith they could obtain heavenly visions, the ministering of angels, have knowledge of the spirits of just men made perfect, of the general assembly and church of the first born, whose names are written in heaven, of God the judge of all, of Jesus the Mediator of the new covenant, and become familiar with the third heavens, see and hear things which were not only unutterable, but were unlawful to utter. Peter, in view of the power of faith, second epistle, first chapter, second and third verses, says to the Former-day Saints: "Grace and peace be multiplied unto you, through the knowledge of God, and of Jesus our Lord, according as his divine power hath given unto us all things that pertain unto life and godliness, through the knowledge of him that hath called us to glory and virtue." In the first epistle, first chapter, third, fourth and fifth verses he says: "Blessed be the God and Father of our Lord Jesus Christ, which, according to his abundant mercy, hath begotten us again unto a lively hope by the resurrection of Jesus Christ from the dead, to

3

an inheritance incorruptible and undefiled, and that fadeth not away, reserved in heaven for you, who are kept by the power of God through faith unto salvation, ready to be revealed in the last time."

18. These sayings put together show the apostle's views most clearly, so as to admit of no mistake on the mind of any individual. He says that all things that pertain to life and godliness were given unto them through the knowledge of God and our Saviour Jesus Christ. And if the question is asked, how were they to obtain the knowledge of God? (for there is a great difference between believing in God and knowing him—knowledge implies more than faith. And notice, that all things that pertain to life and godliness were given through the knowledge of God) the answer is given—through faith they were to obtain this knowledge; and, having power by faith to obtain the knowledge of God, they could with it obtain all other things which pertain to life and godliness.

19. By these sayings of the apostle, we learn that it was by obtaining a knowledge of God that men got the knowledge of all things which pertain to life and godliness, and this knowledge was the effect of faith; so that all things which pertain to life and godliness are the effects of faith.

20. From this we may extend as far as any circumstances may require, whether on earth or in heaven, and we will find it the testimony of all inspired men, or heavenly messengers, that all things that pertain to life and godliness are the effects of faith and nothing else; all learning, wisdom and prudence fail, and every thing else as a means of salvation but faith. This is the reason that the fishermen of Galilee could teach the world— because they sought by faith, and by faith obtained. And this is the reason that Paul counted all things but filth and dross—what he formerly called his gain he called his loss; yea, and he counted all things but loss for the excellency of the knowledge of Christ Jesus the Lord. Philippians iii. 7, 8, 9, and 10. Because to obtain the faith by which he could enjoy the knowledge of Christ Jesus the Lord, he had to suffer the loss of all things. This is the reason that the Former-day Saints knew more, and understood more, of heaven and of heavenly things than all others beside, because this information is the effect of faith—to be obtained by no other means. And this is the reason that men, as soon as they lose their faith, run into strifes, contentions, darkness, and diffi-

culties; for the knowledge which tends to life disappears with faith, but returns when faith returns; for when faith comes it brings its train of attendants with it—apostles, prophets, evangelists, pastors, teachers, gifts, wisdom, knowledge, miracles, healings, tongues, interpretation of tongues, etc. All these appear when faith appears on the earth, and disappear when it disappears from the earth; for these are the effects of faith, and always have attended, and always will, attend it. For where faith is, there will the knowledge of God be also, with all things which pertain thereto—revelations, visions, and dreams, as well as every necessary thing, in order that the possessors of faith may be perfected, and obtain salvation; for God must change, otherwise faith will prevail with him. And he who possesses it will, through it, obtain all necessary knowledge and wisdom, until he shall know God, and the Lord Jesus Christ, whom he has sent whom to know is eternal life. Amen.

(Continued from page 60)

ceivable relation to TIME OR SPACE! O, blush for modern christianity!—a pious name for Atheism! Some, perhaps, may think that I have not sufficient charity. But why should I have charity for a god that has no "parts"—no relation to space? Let him first have charity for himself. But this would be impossible; for he is a god "without passions." He can have no charity nor love for himself nor any one else. There is no danger of offending him; for a passionless god is not capable of anger. One of the persons of this imaginary god is said to have been crucified. But this must be a sad mistake; for it would be impossible to crucify a portion of something that had no "parts." The reason, then, why the people have not received any word from the Great King, is because they have petitioned the wrong god. Would you expect her majesty, the queen of England, to answer your petition if it were directed to some African prince? Would you expect the God of heaven to answer a petition that was addressed to a Hindoo god? If, then, your petitions are addressed to the bodiless, passionless god of modern christianity, you must not be surprised if the true God does not pay any attention to them. You need not expect that the True God will make any reply to petitions offered to any other being.—By Orson Pratt, *The Kingdom of God*, No. 2, pp. 3-4, Liverpool, Oct. 31, 1848.

TRUE FAITH

ORSON PRATT

FAITH THE RESULT OF EVIDENCE—JUSTIFICATION BY FAITH WITH-
OUT WORKS — JUSTIFICATION BY FAITH WITH WORKS — FAITH
THE GIFT OF GOD—MIRACULOUS SIGNS ACCOMPANY TRUE FAITH
IN ALL AGES — WHEN THE SIGNS CEASE, FAITH AND SALVA-
TION CEASE.

1.—It is the intention of the author in this chapter to define
and simplify the great principle, called FAITH.   This is not an
abstract principle, separate and distinct from mind, but it is a
certain condition or state of the mind itself.   When the mind believes or has confidence in any subject, or statement, or proposition, whether correct or incorrect, it is then in possession of
faith.   To have faith is simply to believe.   Faith and belief, therefore, are synonymous terms, expressive of the same idea.

2.—Faith or belief is the result of evidence presented to the
mind.   Without evidence, the mind cannot have faith in anything.
We believe that a stone will fall, when unsupported, on the evidence of past observation in relation to the falling of heavy bodies.
We believe that day and night will continue on the evidence of
past experience in regard to the uniformity of nature's laws.   We
believe that space is boundless, and duration endless, on the evidence, presented by the mind itself, which at once perceives the
absurdity of either space or duration being limited.   We believe
in all self-evident truths, on the evidence that all opposite propo-
sitions to these truths are absurd.   We believe in all the great truths
of science, either on the evidences of our own investigations, or on
the researches of others.   We believe in historical facts on the
evidence of the historian.   Faith in every fact, statement, truth,
or proposition which we have confidence in, is, in all cases whatsoever, derived from evidence.   Therefore, without evidence, faith
can have no existence.

3.—Faith is of two kinds, namely *false* and *true*.   A false faith is
the result of giving credence to false evidence: a true faith, the
result derived from true evidence.

4.—The faith of Cain in offering the fruits of the ground was false, derived from some incorrect evidence, in relation to offerings, or in relation to the conduct necessary to obtain a blessing. The faith of Abel in offering the firstlings of his flock, was founded upon the evidence he had from the word of God that such an offering would please Him. The faith of the Egyptians in the doctrines of the magicians was the result of false evidence, strengthened, and as they supposed, confirmed by the numerous miracles wrought by their evil hands. The faith of Israel in the doctrines of Moses was founded upon true evidence, and hence, was pleasing in the sight of God. Faith in idols and in the mythologies of the heathen, is the result of a false traditionary evidence. Faith in the true God is founded upon true evidence. Faith in false doctrines, and in the creeds and articles of religion, invented by human wisdom, is the production of traditionary evidence, not to be depended on. Faith in every word of God, whether ancient or depended on. Faith in every word of God, whether ancient or modern, is always produced by evidence that is true, and calculated to give the greatest assurance to the mind.

5.—As evidence precedes faith, the latter should be weak or strong in proportion to the weakness or strength of the evidence. Where the evidence is accompanied by circumstances of a doubtful nature; or where it relates to things which are, in some degree, improbable in themselves; or where there is an opposing evidence of nearly the same influence or weight; or where there in only circumstantial evidence—faith should be weak. On the other hand, where the evidences are direct; where they relate to events or things, not improbable; where they are accompanied by favourable circumstances of a confirmatory nature; where no evidences, of any influence or weight, are in opposition—faith should be strong. The weakness or strength of faith will, therefore, in all cases, be in proportion to the weakness or strength of the impressions, produced upon the mind by evidence. It is often the case, that the judgment becomes so weak and beclouded, that the evidences, however great, and clear, and lucid, and demonstrative, produces no sensible impression upon the mind. Hence, faith does not always exist in impaired or vitiated minds with a strength proportioned to the degree or force of evidence.

6.—In our examination into the truth or falsehood of many subjects, we are exceedingly liable to be deceived. Man, through the influence of sophistry, or popularity, or surrounding circumstances or tradition, or many causes, combined, may be biased in his judgment, partial in his investigations, and swayed from that searching analysis which is sometimes requisite in order to discover the truth or error of the subject, statement, or proposition, under consideration. Even his own senses, uncorrected by his judgment, often lead him astray. For instance; a man, looking through the cabin window of a vessel, perceives another vessel apparently moving. He hastily concludes that the other vessel is really in motion, while his own is standing still. In this, he is very liable to be deceived; for the fact may be directly opposite to the one he so hastily assumes; that is, his own vessel may be moving, though imperceptibly to him, while the one at the distance may be standing still; or the phenomenon may be occasioned, by the combined motion of both vessels. All the inhabitants of our globe were for many centuries, deceived in regard to the motions of the heavenly bodies. They believed that the sun, moon, planets, and stars, revolved around the earth daily, until Copernicus undeceived them by proving that the appearances were the result of the simple diurnal rotation of the earth.

7.—Very many have been the deceptions palmed upon the world, under the names of science, theories, hypotheses, doctrines, &c. Hundreds of millions in all ages have been under the influence of false faiths, built upon false evidences. Among all the antediluvian world in the days of the flood, only eight persons had the true faith; all the rest perished with a false faith. In the cities of the plains which were overthrown, Lot and his two daughters were the only ones, having a true faith. Modern Christendom or the nations of great Babylon, have, for centuries, been under the influence of false faiths which will soon lead them to utter destruction.

8.—A false faith in regard to history, science, and many other subjects, is not so injurious to individuals and nations, as an incorrect faith in regard to the doctrine of salvation. To believe that a revelation or message, sent from God, is false, is attended with the most fearful consequences, involving the present and future happiness of the soul. So likewise, to believe human creeds and articles of religion, invented by uninspired men, to be of divine origin, is equally dangerous and fatal in its consequences.

9.—Faith most generally inspires the heart to actions or works of a nature similar and suitable to the belief. Faith in idolatrous systems leads to idolatrous works. Faith in false doctrines leads to false or wicked practices. Faith in the corrupt man-made systems of modern Christianity leads to many corrupt, abominable, and wicked works. Faith in a divine message or new revelation will lead to works in accordance with the requirements contained therein.

10.—When faith, either true or false, is sufficiently powerful to lead to action, it produces effects characteristic of the cause. The faith of Paul, that Jesus of Nazareth was an imposter, led him to persecute his followers with great zeal. Afterwards his faith that Jesus was the son of God, led him to endure all kinds of hardships for his sake. The faith of some led them to really suppose they were doing God service to kill the Apostles. The faith of others made them willing to die for their testimony concerning Jesus. The murderers of the Apostles, and the Apostles themselves, both had faith and works; both were sincere; the one having the false faith and wicked works; the other having true faith and righteous works.

11.—Faith alone will not save men: neither will faith and works save them, unless they are of the right kind. Indeed the faith and works of the greatest portion of mankind will be the very cause of their damnation. True faith and righteous works are essential to salvation; and without both of these, no man ever was, or ever can be saved.

12.—Unless the true principles of salvation be revealed and established by sufficient evidence, there could be no true faith and works by which mankind could obtain salvation; for in the system of salvation, works follow faith, and faith follows evidence and evidence accompanies the revealed truth. For instance, God reveals the great and sublime truths contained in the Book of Mormon Next, He sends evidence sufficient to convince mankind of the divine authenticity of these truths. Thirdly, this evidence produces faith in the minds of those who candidly and carefully examine it. Fourthly, this faith will lead the honest to do the works required of them in that book. And lastly, through the atonement of Christ, these faith and works, combined together, will surely save them in the kingdom of God.

13.—The evidence which God always gives to establish the divinity of His revelations, is sufficient to produce faith in the heart of every person living, who examines it in a proper manner. Hence every creature in all the world, who has come to years of understanding, and who has evidence placed within his reach, is condemned if he does not believe it. There are some who say that, if the evidence were sufficient, they would be compelled to believe; but this is not true—the evidence may be sufficient, and yet they may refuse to examine it; or they may examine it with prejudiced minds, or they may be careless in their examinations, or they may refuse to examine it in the manner in which God has directed; or they may examine it with a determination not to embrace it, even though it be true; or they may be partial in weighing the evidence for, and apparently against it, with a most anxious desire and hope that they shall find it false. All these obstacles, and many others that might be named, prevent them from believing that which an honest, candid, unprejudiced, and prayerful mind would believe. Therefore it is not for the lack of evidence that they disbelieve, but it is their own evil hearts, and the darkness which they bring with them in their investigation. When God reveals a truth, as it is always accompanied with sufficient evidence, all people, because of their agency, can believe or disbelieve it, as they choose: and if they believe it, they can also obey or disobey it, as they choose: and herein is the condemnation of man, because they prefer unbelief to faith, and disobedience to obedience.

14.—When the Apostles were commanded to go into all the world and preach the Gospel to every creature, they were informed that he who believed the Gospel, and was baptized, should be saved, and he who believed not should be damned. To believe the Gospel, as the Apostles preached it, was not sufficient, but Jesus added the condition of baptism, clearly showing that their faith must be manifested by the works, otherwise it would be of no benefit to them. Jesus very well understood that the works necessary to salvation never would be performed without faith, which always precedes them; and, as this faith was in their power to obtain through the evidence offered by the preaching of his Apostles, he determined to damn every creature in all the world that would not believe the message they taught.

15.—There are some who believe that faith alone, unaccompanied by works, is sufficient for justification, sanctification, and salvation. But what would it benefit a hungry man, in a field, who believes that in the house there is a table spread for him with an abundance of food, if he make no exertion to approach the house and obtain the blessing? What profit would it be to a rich man who has faith in the words of Jesus, concerning the feeding of the hungry and the clothing of the naked, unless he have works

corresponding to that faith? What blessing would be obtained
by believing the words which Christ has spoken, unless we do
them? It is not the person who merely believes in the sayings
of Christ, that is justified, but it is he who shows his faith by
obeying them. When Jesus speaks of believers, he has reference,
most generally, to those whose faith has been sufficiently strong
to lead them to obedience. It is to this kind of believers that He
refers in the following passages: "Verily, verily, I say unto you,
he that heareth my words, and believeth on him that sent me, hath
everlasting life, and shall not come into condemnation; but is
passed from death unto life." "For God so loved the world, that
he gave his only begotten Son, that whosoever believeth in him
should not perish, but have everlasting life." "He that believeth
on him is not condemned."

16.—Jesus here refers to a class of believers who should fully
prove their faith by their obedience. Such, and such alone, should
be freed from condemnation—should pass from death unto life—
should become the children of God by having a faith that would
lead them to obey. All other believers are without justification—
without hope—without everlasting life, and will be damned, the
same as unbelievers, because they profess to believe on the words
of the Son of God, but will not obey them.

17.—Jesus says, "If a man love me he will keep my words;
and my Father will love him, and we will come unto him, and
make our abode with him. He that loveth me not keepeth not my
sayings." As a man's love is manifested by his works, so is his
faith.

18.—John says that, "Whosoever believeth that Jesus is the
Christ, is born of God." It is evident, from the whole Epistle in
which these words are contained, that none were to be considered
as really believing that Jesus was the Christ, only those who manifested it by keeping his commandments; for he further says,
"Hereby we do know that we know him, if we keep his commandments. He that saith, I know him, and keepeth not his commandments, is a liar, and the truth is not in him. But whoso keepeth
his word, in him verily is the love of God perfected: hereby know
that we are in him." And again, he says, "Every one that doeth
righteousness is born of him." "Whosoever doeth not righteousness is not of God." "He that keepeth his commandments dwelleth
in him, and he in him." "Every one that loveth is born of God,
and knoweth God." "He that loveth not, knoweth not God; for

God is love." "He that dwelleth in love, dwelleth in God, and God in him. Herein is our love made perfect, that we may have boldness in the day of judgment; because, as he is, so are we in this world. There is no fear in love, but perfect love casteth out fear; because fear hath torment. He that feareth is not made perfect in love. We love him, because he first loved us." "This is the love of God, that we keep his commandments; and his commandments are not grievous."

19.—From all these passages it is easy to perceive that salvation depends upon our loving God; and that loving God is the keeping of His commandments; and the keeping of His commandments is the only sure evidence of our really believing that Jesus is the Christ. Let no persons, therefore, flatter or deceive themselves with the idea that they believe from their heart, that Jesus is the Christ, or that they are born of God, or that they have passed from death unto life, or that they love God, unless they are certain that they have kept His commandments and sayings. Millions are deceiving themselves with a false faith and with a false hope — deluding themselves with the notion that they are born of God, when they have not attended even to the first commandments in relation to their adoption. All such will meet with a bitter disappointment.

20.—The first effect of true faith is a sincere, true, and thorough repentance of all sins; the second effect is an immersion in water, for the remission of sins; the third is the reception of the ordinance of the laying on of the hands for the baptism of the Holy Ghost: these are the first commandments in the Gospel. No man has a saving faith without attending to these three requirements. No person can be a believer in Christ, in the scriptural sense of that term, without complying, in the strictest manner, with these commandments; without receiving these, it will be in vain for him to pray for a forgiveness of sins, or for the baptism of the Spirit, or for salvation: and if he flatters himself that he loves God, or that he can obtain eternal life without obeying these first commandments, he is woefully deceived. Indeed these are the introductory principles, and the only principles by which men and women can be born into the kingdom of Christ, and become his sons and daughters. After attending to these, there are other commandments for them to obey; but if they undertake to obey the others first, they will find their endeavors unacceptable in the sight of God. For instance, God requires His sons and daugh-

ters to keep the Sabbath day holy; but no man can keep the
Sabbath holy until he has attended to the first three commandments of the Gospel, after which he can keep the Sabbath according to the mind of God, but not before. There are many commandments which none but those who are born of God can keep.
And for a man to undertake to keep them before attending to the
first three, would be like a child's undertaking to read before it
had learned the alphabet.

21.—A faith, then, that brings remission of sins or justification
to the sinner, is that which is connected with repentance and baptism. Faith alone will not justify; faith and baptism alone
will not justify; but faith, repentance, and baptism will justify
and bring remission of sins through the blood of Christ. What
does Paul mean when he says, "Therefore being justified by
faith, we have peace with God, through our Lord Jesus
Christ?" He means that faith is the starting point — the
foundation and cause of our repentance and baptism which bring
remission or justification; and being the cause which leads to
those results, it is not improper to impute justification to faith.
What does that Scripture mean which says, "If thou shalt confess
with thy mouth the Lord Jesus, and shalt believe in thine heart
that God hath raised him from the dead, thou shalt be saved.
For with the heart man believeth unto righteousness, and with the
mouth confession is made unto salvation?" It means that real faith
in the heart is that which leads to obedience; for a man who does
not obey, only has a degree of faith, and not living faith in the
heart, which in all cases will lead to repentance, confession, baptism, laying on of hands, &c. All will admit that to believe with
the heart leads to and includes repentance. Why not also admit
that it includes every other commandment of the Gospel? Because believng with the heart in the resurrection of Christ is the
moving cause of obedience which brings salvation, it well may be
said that salvation is the result of faith.

22.—There has been much dispute among mankind in regard
to justification. Some have supposed that we are justified by the
blood of Christ by simple faith alone, without performing any
works either of the law or Gospel. Others suppose that we are
justified by the blood of Christ by simply adding repentance to
our faith without any further works. Others contend that all
mankind will be justified and saved through the blood of Christ,
without either faith or works. All these admit that the atonement

of Christ is necessary to justification. The only dispute seems to be in regard to the conditions required of the creature by which he receives the justification purchased by the atonement. Those who believe that simple faith alone, without works, is the only condition required, generally urge the following passages in support of that view; "For if Abraham were justified by works, he hath whereof to glory; but not before God. For what saith the Scripture? Abraham believed God, and it was counted unto him for righteousness. Now to him that worketh is the reward not reckoned of grace, but of debt. But to him that worketh not, but believeth on him that justifieth the ungodly, his faith is counted for righteousness. Even as David also describeth the man, unto whom God imputeth righteousness without works." (Rom. iv. 2--6) Those who believe works necessary to justification, quote the following: "What doth it profit, my brethren, though a man say he have faith, and have not works? Can faith save him? "Faith, if it hath not works, is dead, being alone. Yea, a man may say, Thou hast faith and I have works: show me thy faith without thy works, and I will show thee my faith by my works. Thou believest that there is one God; thou doest well: the devils also believe and tremble. But wilt thou know, O vain man, that faith without works is dead? Was not Abraham, our father, justified by works, when he had offered Isaac, his son upon the altar? Seest thou how faith wrought with his works, and by works was faith made perfect? And the Scripture was fulfilled which saith, Abraham believed God, and it was imputed unto him for righteousness: and he was called the Friend of God. Ye see then how that by works a man is justified, and not by faith only. Likewise also was not Rahab, the harlot, justified by works, when she had received the messengers, and had sent them out another way? For as the body without the Spirit is dead, so faith without works, is dead also." (James ii. 14—26.) Paul and James seem apparently to contradict each other; and this has been the cause of differences of opinion in our day: but these apparent contradictions can easily be reconciled, if we take into consideration the two different subjects upon which they were writing. Paul was writing to a people who were inclined to believe in circumcision, and other works of the ancient law had been done away in Christ. And he shows clearly that circumcision and many of those ancient laws were given in the earlier ages, not to take away past sins, nor to justify those to whom they were given, but for various other purposes:

and that by complying with those works, they did nothing more than what they were indebted to do, and that the reward attached to these acts was "not reckoned of grace, but of debt;" or, in other words, the reward of grace is a forgiveness of past sins; but the reward of debt is a freedom from the condemnation, not of past sins, but of the sins which would exist in the case we refused to pay the debt: for instance, God commanded Abraham to circumcise himself and all the males of his house, not to justify himself or his house of past sins, but for another purpose. When this commandment was given, it brought Abraham under obligation to obey it; it was a debt he owed to the Lord; if he paid it, there would be no condemnations arising from disobedience in relation to that particular commandment, and he would have the reward of a clear conscience, so far as the payment of that particular debt was concerned; but in all this there is no reward of grace manifested in the forgiveness of any sins which may have previously been committed. Therefore as obedience to these particular laws did not bring remission of sins, Paul could with propriety say that Abraham and others were not justified by works, that is, by such works of the law as circumcision, &c., which were given for a very different purpose than that of justification . It was very necessary that Abraham should do those works, though they were not works intended to bring remission of sins or justification, yet the performance of them would prevent the sin of negligence, and would also bring such blessings as were attached to them by way of promise. But after these laws and circumcision were done away in Christ, then Paul could say, "But to him that worketh not, but believeth on him that justifieth the ungodly, his faith is counted for righteousness." If those laws and ordinances which were given to Abraham to perform, were not intended to justify him of his past sins, much less would they justify those who lived after Christ when they were done away. After Christ, these works given to Abraham to perform, were not considered even as a debt binding upon any: they were works, therefore, that would be sinful to perform. The faith of that man that "worketh not," that is, that does not perform works that are done away, "is counted for righteousness."

23.—But as Abraham was justified by faith, it may not be improper to inquire whether there were any other class of works, connected with his faith, that were of a justifying nature. Paul says, "The Scripture foreseeing that God would justify the heath-

en through faith, preached before the Gospel unto Abraham saying: In thee shall all nations be blest."—(Gal. iii. 8.) From this
we learn that the same Gospel that was to justify the heathen
through faith, and bless all nations, was actually preached to
Abrham.   Now in the Gospel there are certain works to be connected with faith for justification: by these works of the Gospel,
he manifested his faith and obtained justification: and not by the
works of the law, such as circumcision, &c. Paul says, "Faith
was reckoned to Abraham for righteousness. How was it then reckoned? when he was in circumcision or in uncircumcision?   Not
in circumcision, but in uncircumcision.   And he received the
sign of circumcision, a seal of the righteousness of the faith
which he had, yet being uncircumcised: that he might be
the father of all them that believe, though they be not circumcised:
that righteousness might be imputed unto them also; and the
father of circumcision to them who are not of the circumcision
only, but who also walk in the steps of that faith of our father
Abraham, which he had being yet uncircumcised.—(Rom.iv. 9—
12.) From these passages we learn, that Abraham was justified
before circumcision, consequently the Gospel of justification must
have been preached to him before that law was given.   That
there were works connected with the Gospel preached to Abraham, is evident from the fact that all the heathen nations who
lived in the Apostles' days, could be justified and become his
children by walking, as Paul says, "in the steps of that faith of
our father Abraham." There were certain steps pertaining to the
Gospel and faith of Abraham, in which he walked; otherwise
he could not have been justified.   Whatever works these steps
of justification included, the very same were required of the
heathen after Christ.   These steps of the Gospel, since Christ,
we have already observed, are Repentance and Baptism, which
bring remission of sins and justification, being the results of
faith, or, in other words, the steps of faith that Abraham walked
in.   Therefore, "to him that worketh not" the works of circumcision and other laws that are done away, but performeth the
works of the Gospel, "his faith is counted for righteousness,"
the same as Abraham's was, who walked in the steps of the same
Gospel, and was justified in the same way.   This view of the
subject perfectly reconciles the teachings of both Paul and James,
and shows most clearly that both were correct, when their state-
ments are applied to the two different subjects upon which they
were writing.

24.—Faith is the gift of God. In what manner does God give faith? Does He impart this gift to the mind by the immediate operation of the Holy Spirit independent of any other means? Does He bestow it unsought for and irrespective of the preparation of the mind? Does He confer it independent of the agency of man? To say that man obtains this gift without preparing himself, or without the exercise of any agency, is to deprive him of all responsibility in regard to whether he has faith or not. This condition would free him from all blame or condemnation for unbelief. If agency is in no way concerned in obtaining faith, it would be the highest act of injustice to punish the unbeliever: there would be no more responsibility about him than there is about the dumb brute. What would be thought of the justice of a man who would punish his horse because he was not harnessed? If the animal were endowed with the power of speech, would he not say that he was an irresponsible being, that he had no power or agency to harness himself, that the gift of harnessing belonged to a higher and superior being to himself, and that he considered it very cruel, and unjust, and tyrannical for that higher being to punish him for not exercising a faculty with which he was not endowed, which was far beyond his capacities, and which was a condition that man alone was capable of bestowing? If faith is the gift of God, and man has no agency in obtaining this gift, then he stands in the same relation to God in regard to having faith, as the horse does to the man in regard to being harnessed; and if it would be unjust and cruel in man to punish his horse for not being harnessed, it would be equally unjust and cruel for God to punish man for not having faith, if he be considered a being incapable of the exercise of such a faculty.

25.—That faith is the gift of God there is no dispute; but that God bestows this gift unsought for, and without any preparation or agency on the part of man, is not only unscriptural and unreasonable, but extremely absurd, when we consider that man is to be punished for his unbelief. But some may inquire, has not God the power and right to do with man as He pleases? Has not He power to withhold faith, and punish whomsoever He will, whether they deserve it or not? We reply that whatever power God has, it is certain that He will not exercise it contrary to the principles of Justice and Mercy, or contrary to the revealed character which He has given of Himself. If it were possible for

Him to change or deviate from His word, then He would cease
to be God. If He would punish the innocent and acquit the
guilty, He would be a Being altogether unlovely and undesirable
—a Being to be feared, but not to be loved. Therefore we may
rest assured that He will never punish a man for his unbelief,
unless man has the power to obtain faith through the exercise
of his own free will.

26.—But if faith cannot be obtained, unless sought for properly, how can the sayings of Paul to the Ephesians be reconciled
with this idea? "For by grace are ye saved through faith; and
that not of yourselves; it is the gift of God; not of works, lest
any man should boast. For we are His workmanship, created
in Christ Jesus unto good works, which God hath before ordained that we should walk in them."—(Eph. ii. 8—10). We
are to understand from these passages, that the grace and faith
by which man is saved, are the gifts of God, having been purchased for him not by his own works, but by the blood of Christ.
Had not these gifts been purchased for man, all exertions on his
part would have been entirely unavailing and fruitless. Whatever
course man might have pursued, he could not have atoned for
one sin; it required the sacrifice of a sinless and pure Being in
order to purchase the gifts of faith, repentance, and salvation
for fallen man. Grace, Faith, Repentance, and Salvation, when
considered in their origin, are not of man, neither by his works;
man did not devise, originate, nor adopt them; superior Beings
in Celestial abodes, provided these gifts, and revealed the conditions to man by which he might become a partaker of them.
Therefore all boasting on the part of man is excluded. He is
saved by a plan which his works did not originate—a plan of
heaven, and not of earth.

27.—Well might the Apostle declare to the Ephesians, that
these gifts were not of themselves, neither of their works, when
the God and Father of our spirits, from whom cometh every
good and perfect gift, was the great Author of them. But are
these great gifts bestowed on fallen man without his works? No:
man has these gifts purchased for and offered to him; but before
he can receive and enjoy them he must exercise his agency and
accept of them: and herein is the condemnation of man, because
when he was in a helpless fallen condition, and could not by
his own works and devices atone for the least of his sins, the
only Begotten of the Father gave his own life to purchase the

gifts of faith and salvation for him, and yet he will not so much as accept of them.

28.—Faith therefore is the gift of God, but man cannot have this choice heavenly treasure only in God's own appointed way. Among the means that God has ordained through which man may receive this great and precious gift, may be mentioned the preaching of the word by men called and inspired by the gift and power of the Holy Ghost: for saith the Apostle, "How then shall they call on him in whom they have not believed? And how shall they believe in him of whom they have not heard? And how shall they hear without a preacher? And how shall they preach except they be sent?" "So then, faith cometh by hearing, and hearing by the word of God."—(Rom. x. 14, 15, 17.) Though faith be the gift of God, yet it comes by hearing the word. Through this medium man makes himself acquainted with the evidence in favour of the divinity of the word; the evidence being of divine origin as well as the word. This evidence begets faith in the mind; and this faith, though it be obtained through the exercise of the free will and agency of the creature, is still the gift of God, granted through the evidence accompanying the preached word. In the Apostles' days, when the art of printing was unknown, and the great majority of mankind could not read the word, the principle means of obtaining faith was by the process of preaching and hearing, but in these days, in many instances, faith comes by reading as well as by preaching: for a man called and inspired of God can both preach and write by the power of the Holy Ghost, and when the honest humble soul either hears or reads that which is given by the Spirit, the light that is in him witnesseth that it is of God; for light cleaves to light, and truth to truth; the Spirit gives light to every man that comes into the world, and if he loves the light that is in himself, he will love all other light that is presented to his mind, and embrace it. Light cannot be presented to the mind of a candid, honest person, without being perceived to be light; but if he receive it not he extinguishes in a degree the light that is in him, and darkness still greater ensues, and he is left to commit evils of a greater magnitude, until the light that was in him has entirely fled, and darkness reigns triumphantly: this darkness brings misery and wretchedness in this world and eternal torment in the world to come. This is the state of man who rejects light and truth, and will not exercise faith in that which the light that is in him teaches him is truth.

29.—The word and the evidence accompanying it are both the gifts of God; but besides these, the light that is in every man who comes into the world is also the gift of God through Christ. For if Christ had not purchased this gift for man by his atoning blood, man would have been destitute of all light. Darkness alone would have reigned, and our world would have been a hell— the miserable abode of fallen spirits and fallen man: no ray of light could have penetrated the darkened understanding: the extreme of misery would have been the result. But saith our Saviour, "I am the light and the life of the world;" all light that is in the world came by him through his atonement; it is the gift of God to fallen man. If the light that is in man be the gift of God, surely all additional light offered to him, must be the gift of God also. By faith man should lay hold of this light, wherever he may discover it.

30.—The only way to receive additional faith and light is to practise according to the light which we have: and if we do this, we have the promise of God that the same shall grow brighter and brighter until the perfect day. Every word of God is light and truth. He that saith, that he is in the light, but obeyeth not the words of truth, is deceiving himself, and is in darkness; for none are the children of faith except such as walk in the light, and obey its laws. How many millions in Christendom profess to be Christians, and say that they are in the light and have been born of God, and yet they have never obeyed even the first principles of the light; they have never repented properly and been immersed in water for the remission of sins by the ministration of one whom God has authorized; and yet they pretend that God for Christ's sake has forgiven their sins. How blindly deceived! and how vain their faith and hope of salvation! God has not forgiven their sins; neither will He forgive them, until they obey the message of the Gospel according to the precise order which He has revealed. Faith is the gift of God, and is one of the means of salvation; but none can have this gift except in the way that God has ordained: and all who pretend to have faith and obey not that form of doctrine which God has revealed will find that their faith is of no effect, and that they will be damned with unbelievers: for God will not confer saving gifts upon the disobedient.

31.—Every thing that is good comes from God and is the gift of God. God has given revelation upon revelation unto man for his benefit; and the generations to whom He has given His word will be judged by that word at the last day. God raised up a prophet in our day, and gave him the Urim and Thummim, and revealed a flood of light and truth through him to this generation. This generation will be judged out of the books and revelations which God gave through this prophet. If they exercise faith in these revelations, and obey the same, they will be justified and saved; but if they disbelieve them, and harden their hearts against them, they will surely be damned; for the Almighty reveals not His word in vain. What doth it benefit this generation to offer them a heavenly gift, and reveal to them more light and truth if they receive it not? The gift benefits those only who receive it. The rest will receive a greater condemnation. When the honest read that heavenly treasure—the Book of Mormon, they are filled with joy unspeakable, because God has again spoken to man as in ancient times; their souls feast upon the contents of that holy and divine book; and so great is their joy, that they cannot find language adequate to express the overflowings of their hearts. But how different are the feelings of those who reject it; light and truth flee from them, and they feel angry to think that God should again speak to man. But God will show them by His Almighty power that His word cannot be rejected with impunity. The judgments that have befallen ancient generations and nations who have rejected His word, ought to be a solemn warning to those now on the earth. But alas! the pride, high-mindedness, and great wickedness of man cause him to hate the light because his deeds are evil. And thus this generation will, for the most part, perish in unbelief and disobedience to one of the greatest and most important messages that God ever sent for the salvation of the people. Oh, poor fallen man! how eager for happiness, and yet how unwilling to receive it upon righteous principles! Oh, that thou didst but know the day of thy visitation and wouldst incline thine ear and hearken to the voice of God and harden not thy heart for then it would be well with thee! But thou knowest not, neither dost thou consider the fearful judgments that await thee, if thou turnest a deaf ear to the last great message of mercy, now revealed from the heavens, for thy good! Oh, turn unto the Lord, and exercise faith in Him, that thy light and joy may be increased—thy faith and love become perfected, that all of the gifts of God may abound in thee, that thou mayest finally obtain eternal life, which is the greatest of all the gifts of God to man.

32.—Without true and genuine faith it is impossible to please God; and Jesus expressly says, that "He that believeth not shall be damned." It is of the utmost importance, therefore, that every man examines himself in the most careful and rigid manner to see whether he be in the faith or not. The only sure and perfect standard with which to compare his faith is the word and Spirit of God.

33.—Reader, are you sincerely desiring salvation, and do you wish to enter into a most thorough and searching examination of your faith? Are you willing to have your faith compared with and measured by the divine oracles? Are you a believer in the word of God? If so, you must be aware, that you are commanded in the most emphatic terms, to repent of all your sins. This is the very first act required of a Bible believer. Have you repented sincerely, and humbly, and with all your heart? Have you confessed all your sins unto God with a broken heart and contrite spirit? Have you, not only confessed, but forsaken every sin? Have you made sufficient acknowledgement and satisfaction to those whom you may have in any way injured? Have you covenanted with and promised the Lord that you will sin no more? If you have not repented in this manner and reformed your conduct, then you are not a true believer; your faith is vain, and your hopes are vain, and you are yet in your sins, not having complied with even the very first requisition of faith.

34.—But, if you have most sincerely repented and put away your evil deeds, then you have taken the *first* permanent step towards a true and saving faith. You are now humble and contrite in your feeling; your heart is tender, and you feel grieved that you have ever sinned against God. You feel determined that henceforth you will reform. You are a believing penitent sinner; and your great desire is to obtain a pardon of your sins. You ask the Lord to forgive you, but He does not grant your request. You pray much, but still you have no evidence that your sins are forgiven. You go forward to be prayed for by your ministers and friends, but find no relief. You become discouraged and perhaps fall back into sin, thinking that there is something wrong, or that there is no hope for you; or perhaps you may be persuaded by your minister that your sins are forgiven, and you try to fancy that it is so; though you have no certainty that you are pardoned, yet you hope that such is the case; this false hope causes you to be somewhat easy in your feelings and you fancy all is well.

35.—But let me tell you plainly that you are deceiving your-self. Your sins are not forgiven. It is true, you have believed the word of God, and have repented; but repentance is only the first step towards obtaining forgiveness. You have another great step to take, before you can expect your sins to be pardoned. You must be immersed in water, by one having authority from God, in the name of the Father, and of the Son, and of the Holy Ghost, for the remission of your sins. Then, and not till then, your sins will be forgiven; for these are the two grand steps, to be joined with your faith, in order that your sins may be washed away, by the atoning blood of Christ. Faith, without repentance and baptism, will not bring you pardon; neither will repentance bring you forgiveness; neither will faith and repent-ance, both together, be sufficient to bring remission of sins; but Faith, Repentance, and Baptism, are sure to put you in possession of a complete justification of all past sins.

36.—Faith leads you to repentance and to the waters of bap-tism for the remission of sins. Faith, connected with repentance alone, is not a justifying faith. In order to be justified by faith, Baptism as well as repentance must be coupled with faith; these three joined in one, constitute the Faith of Justification; where either is wanting, there justification does not exist, and the pen-ient believer is yet in his sins.

37.—Are you, dear Reader, anxious that your sins should all be blotted out? If so, seek not to obtain this choice blessing, contrary to the Gospel: delude not yourself with the vain hope that you are already pardoned, when you have done nothing more than to repent. God will not accept your repentance, unless you be baptized for the remission of your sins. Have you ever gone down into the water and been buried therein, as penitent believers did in ancient times? Have you ever buried the deeds of the old man in a watery grave, as the body of Christ was buried? Did you by such burial, become dead to sin, as Jesus became dead, as it regards his mortal body? Have you ever arisen from the watery tomb to newness of life, as Jesus arose from the tomb of mortality to immortality? Unless you have done this, both your faith and hope are vain.

38.—Again, if you have been immersed by one whom God has not sent, and to whom God has not spoken and given authority to baptize; or if you have been baptized by any one who denies new revelation, and does away any of the miraculous gifts of the Gospel, and says, they are unnecessary in these days, then know assuredly, that your immersion is illegal, and will in no wise be accounted as baptism to you. Therefore your only hope of obtaining pardon will be, to search after one whom the Lord has truly authorized, and receive this sacred ordinance under his hands; and then your sins shall be forgiven you, and you will, so far as these first steps are concerned, have the true genuine Gospel faith.

39.—You have now, by complying with repentance and baptism, been set free from all past sin. You have been born of the water, but not of the spirit. Though justified, you yet lack a most essential and important blessing, namely, The Baptism of the Holy Ghost.

40.—God hath ordained ordinances through which Gospel blessings are granted to believers. We have already stated, that the ordinance of Baptism when ministered by proper authority, is that through which pardon comes to the penitent believer; so likewise, God hath ordained the laying on of the hands of His authorized servants, as the sacred ordinance through which He will bestow upon baptized believers the *Gift of the Holy Ghost.*

41.—The Baptism of the Holy Ghost cannot be dispensed with by the believer, any more than the baptism of water. To be born of the water, only justifies the sinner of past sins; but to be born, afterwards, of the Holy Ghost, sanctifies him and prepares him for spiritual blessings in this life, and for eternal life in the world to come. To be born of the water does not qualify him to enter into the kingdom of God, but to be born, first, of the water, and afterwards, of the spirit, fully qualifies him to enter and dwell in that kingdom. Jesus says, "Verily, verily, I say unto you, except a man be born of the water and of the spirit, he can in no wise enter into the kingdom of God." A man may believe, repent, and be immersed in water, or in other words, be born of water, and yet, according to the word of Jesus, he cannot enter into the kingdom of God, without also being born of the spirit.

42.—The ordinance of the *Laying on of Hands* for the birth of the Spirit, is, therefore, essential to salvation.

43.—The men and women of Samaria were born of the water several days before they were born of the spirit. Peter and John were under the necessity of performing a journey from

Jerusalem to Samaria, to lay hands on the baptized believers of the latter city, that they might also be born of the spirit, even as they had been born of the water several days before.

44.—The baptized believers at Ephesus were born of the spirit through the laying on of the hands of Paul. Paul also was born, first of the water to wash away his sins; (Acts xxii. 16,) and secondly, of the Spirit by the ministration of Ananias. (Acts ix. 17, 18.)

45.—Having by faith received forgiveness of sins, and the gift of the Holy Ghost, the believers begin with greater assurance to lay hold of every blessing promised in the Gospel. They read that certain miraculous signs shall be given to believers. (Mark xvi. 15, 18.) They consider that they have the right to enjoy these signs, according to the promise which Jesus made. And they soon find, that through faith, they, in the name of Jesus, can cast out devils, speak in new tongues, overcome deadly poisons, heal the sick, dream heavenly dreams, see open visions, prophesy of future events, receive revelations, control the powers of nature, and, in short, do anything that is necessary for their welfare and the glory of God. All these blessings are obtained by faith; and without faith no spiritual gifts can be received.

46.—The gift of the Holy Ghost, with all its miraculous powers, is one of the great distinguishing differences between Gospel believers and unbelievers. Jesus has been pleased to promise to the one class miraculous signs, and to the other damnation. All persons who wish to thoroughly examine their faith by the word of God, can at once determine to which of these two classes they belong. All who find themselves in possession of the signs, know of a surety that they are believers, and consequently subjects of salvation. But all who find themselves destitute of these signs, know at once, that they are unbelievers, and, therefore, subjects of damnation.

47.—The nations of apostate Christendom are deceiving themselves with the vain and foolish idea, that they are Gospel believers, without the promised accompanying signs. They suppose that they have the true faith without enjoying the promised miraculous effects of that faith; thus they have been deluding themselves with a false faith, and unfounded hope, for some seventeen centuries past. Where faith exists, these miraculous signs exist. If the signs have ceased, then faith has ceased also.

Without these signs, no church, either Catholic or Protestant, can be saved; for they are not believers.

48.—Faith, though the gift of God, is not only obtained by the exercise of the agency of man, but is also increased and perfected by the same agency. Obedience to the ancient Gospel will necessarily impart the ancient Faith: and Faith will necessarily have the same power to prevail with God, in one age as in another. If, through Repentance, Baptism, and Laying on of Hands, in ancient times, Faith was so increased as to obtain Remission of Sins, the Gift of the Holy Ghost, and Miraculous Signs, why will not obedience, in this age, to the same three requirements, impart the same degree of Faith? And why not also the same three Gospel blessings, follow the same Faith?

49.—Can any one show any reason, or present any evidence from the divine oracles, why obedience to the ancient Gospel will not give the same Faith now as in ancient times? Will not Repentance, in all ages, have the same moral effect upon the mind? Is not Gospel Baptism now the same as anciently? Is not every step of obedience to the Gospel the same now as ever? All Bible believers will, at once, answer, that every requirement of the Gospel is the same; and that all can still yield the same acceptable obedience to each requirement; this being the case, does it not necessarily follow, that the same obedience will impart the same Faith; and still further, that the same Gospel Faith will bring the same Gospel blessings? Nothing is more certain.

50.—The same Jesus that promised to the believer the Remission of Sins, as a Gospel blessing, also promied to the same believer Miraculous Signs, as Gospel blessings. What authority has the Gospel believer to claim one Gospel blessing, and reject the others? Would not this be indirectly rejecting the whole Gospel? He that offends in one point of the law, is, by our Savior, represented as guilty of the transgression of the whole. He who has no faith to obtain Gospel signs, has no faith to obtain Gospel pardon. He who would thus pervert the Gospel is most woefully deceived, if he supposes himself in possession of any Gospel blessing. Jesus has made no Gospel promises to be trifled with, or to be rejected with impunity by professed believers.

51.—Faith in all ages, and under all dispensations, has always prevailed with God. By faith, signs, miracles, and manifestations of the power of God, were abundantly shown forth under the

Patriarchal, Mosiac, and Christian dispensations. Jesus said, "All things are possible to him that believeth."—(Mark ix. 23.) Again he said, "Have faith in God. For verily I say unto you, That whosoever shall say unto this mountain, Be thou removed, and be thou cast into the sea; and shall not doubt in his heart, but shall believe that those things which he saith shall come to pass; he shall have whatsoever he saith. Therefore I say unto you, what things soever ye desire, when ye pray, believe that ye receive them, and ye shall have them."—(Mark xi. 22, 23, 24.) In another passage He said, "Verily, verily, I say unto you, He that believeth on me, the works that I do shall he do also; and greater works than these shall he do; because I go unto my Father."—(John xiv. 12.)

52.—None of these passages limit the miraculous effects of Faith to the Apostles, or to any particular class of true believers, or to any particular age of the world. But on the contrary; each of these promises was made on the broadest terms, general and unlimited as to time or place. The terms, *"He that believeth;"* *"Whosoever shall say,"* &c., are applicable to all believers, in all ages, and in all the world, unto the latest generations, or to the end of time. No other Gospel blessings were more unlimited in their application. No other more positively and definitely expressed. No other that we have any more right to claim or seek after by Faith.

53.—Indeed, the miraculous gifts were to be the effects—the results—the signs of faith, by which the true believer could, by the most infallible evidence distinguish himself from an unbeliever. By these gifts he is confirmed; and he obtains the most satisfactory knowledge and absolute certainty of the divinity of the doctrine which he has embraced. By these tokens, he knows that he is in reality a true genuine Gospel believer, that his sins are surely forgiven, and that he has received the gift of the Holy Spirit, and is, indeed, an heir of Salvation.

54.—While on the other hand, without these gifts, he knows that he is not a believer—that he has no genuine gospel faith—that he has no claim to any of the other Gospel blessings—that he is classified with unbelievers, and with them he must be damned.

55.—Jesus has made the contrast so great, and the distinguishing marks so apparent, between true and genuine Gospel believers and unbelievers, that it is impossible for any man who examines his own faith by the word of God, to be deceived.

56.—Reader, are you a believer or an unbeliever? Do signs follow you, according to the promise of Jesus in the last chapter of Mark? Have you ever cast out devils in the name of Jesus? Have you ever spoken with another tongue by the power of the Holy Ghost? Have you ever had faith to prevail against deadly poisons? Have you ever healed the sick in the name of Jesus, by the laying on of your hands? Have you ever obtained any of the promised miraculous gifts of the Spirit? If you have not, then you are not a Gospel believer, and are included in that class which Jesus says, shall be damned. Your condition is a fearful one indeed, without the true faith, without hope, without salvation, exposed to the wrath which must fall upon unbelievers.

57.—Do you inquire what you must do? The answer is, become a Bible believer; forsake the false, corrupt, and powerless systems of uninspired men; follow not after any religion because of its popularity; but seek after the faith of the Saints, such as is so clearly defined in the Bible. Seek for the blessings enjoyed by all true believers in Christ; rest not satisfied until you are in possession of the signs of a believer; for know assuredly if you stop short of this, you can in no wise be saved. It is the word which God has spoken, and which He will not revoke.

58.—Now, dear reader, we have plainly pointed out to you the nature of faith; we have proven to you that faith, like all other good things, is the gift of God to man; we have clearly shown you how to obtain a true and genuine Gospel faith; we have also told you how to examine your faith to know whether it be the right kind: we have referred you to the miraculous signs which Jesus says shall follow all believers throughout the world; we have proved that without these signs, there can be no believers, no faith, no Church of Christ, no salvation. And now we close this subject by telling you plainly, that God has again restored His Church to the earth, by revealing the Book of Mormon, containing the everlasting Gospel; by sending His angels as predicted by His servant John on Patmos; by restoring Apostles, and all other officers of the Priesthood; and by setting up His latter-day kingdom, as foretold by Daniel the prophet.

59.—As many as have received this message with all their hearts, have been blessed with the signs promised to believers; and we know of a surety, and bear record that God is the same, faith is the same, the Gospel is the same, and that all the miraculous gifts thereof are the same, as in ancient days; and that the faithful Saints enjoy all blessings now, as in days of old.

60.—Let me earnestly entreat you to break off all your sins, and to bow before your Father in Heaven, and ask Him, if what you have now read is true. If you will do this with a sincere and humble heart, God will manifest the truth of these things to you by the power of the Holy Ghost.

Shem was Melchizedek

From this definite account of driving the "nations apart, when the ancient hills did bow," all reflecting minds may judge that man was scattered over the whole face of the earth. And with the superior knowledge of men like Noah, Shem (who was Melchizedek) and Abraham, the father of the faithful, three cotemporaries, holding the keys of the highest order of the priesthood: connecting the creation, and fall; memorising the righteousness of Enoch; and glorying in the construction of the ark for the salvation of a world; still retaining the model and pattern of that ark, than which a great, ah, we might say, half so great a vessel has never been built since; for another ark, be it remembered, with such a ponderous living freight will never be prepared as a *vessel of mercy* by command of Jehovah.

Times and Seasons, Vol. 5, p. 746.
Nauvoo, Illinois, December 15, 1844. Elder John Taylor, Editor.)

The Faith of Melchizedek

(From Inspired "Translation" of Scriptures, by
Joseph the Prophet.)

Now Melchizedek was a man of faith, who wrought righteousness; and when a child he feared God, and stopped the mouths of lions, and quenched the violence of fire.

And thus, having been approved of God. he was ordained an high priest after the order of the covenant which God made with Enoch.

It being after the order of the Son of God; which order came, not by man, nor the will of man; neither by father nor mother; neither by beginning of days nor end of years; but of God;

And it was delivered unto men by the calling of his own voice, according to his will, unto as many as believed on his name.

For God having sworn unto Enoch and unto his seed with an oath by himself; that every one being ordained after this order and calling should dry up waters, to turn them out of their course;

To put at defiance the armies of nations, to divide the earth; to break every hand, to stand in the presence of God; to do all things according to his will, according to his command, subdue principalities and powers; and this by the will of the Son of God which was from before the foundation of the world.

And men having this faith, coming up unto this order of God, were translated and taken up into heaven.

And now Melchizedek was a priest of this order; therefore he obtained peace in Salem, and was called the prince of peace.

And his people wrought righteousness, and obtained heaven, and sought for the city of Enoch which God had before taken, separating it from the earth, having reserved it unto the latter days, or the end of the world;

And hath said, and sworn with an oath, that the heavens and the earth should come together; and the sons of God should be tried so as by fire.

Genesis 14:26-35.

FROM "MELCHIZEDEK"
By ARIEL L. CROWLEY, LL. B.
CONDENSED RESEARCH BIBLIOGRAPHY OF WORKS CITED AND SOURCES OF QUOTATIONS

ADAM AND MELCHIZEDEK: Vol. 1, Ency. of Freemasonry (Rev. Ed.) Hawkins & Hugha, p. 15.

ALFORD: New Testament for English Readers (1862) on Heb. 7:1-3.

AMERICAN ENCYCLOPEDIA: Vol. 18, p. 603.

AMERICAN STANDARD VERSION: See Heb. 7:1-13.

ANONYMOUS: Five Books vs. Marcion: Book 4, Lines 87-106.

APOCRYPHAL WORKS: "Acts of the Holy Apostles" on Psalms 110:4.

ATHANASIUS: See "Melchizedek" in Baring-Gould's "Legends of the Prophets and Patriarchs."

BARING-GOULD, S,: See "Melchizedek" in his "Legends of the Prephets and Patriarchs."

SYRIAC VERSION: See Heb. 7:1-13 in Murdock's Translation of the Peshitto.

TERTULLIAN: "Answer to the Jews," Chapters 2 and 3; Also Marcion Bk. 5, Ch. 9; and Adv. Haer. Ch. 8.

TESTAMENTS OF THE TWELVE PATRIARCHS: Testament of Levi, Chapter 8 on "New Priesthood."

THEOPHILUS OF ANTIOCH: Epistle to Autolycus, Chapter 31.

THEODOTUS: Fragment preserved in Tertullian Adv. Haer. Chapter 8.

TIMOTHEUS OF CONSTANTINOPLE: De Receptione Haereticorum (Cotelier, Monumento Ecc. Graeca, Book III, p. 392. (See also Pseudo-Tertullian, Praescript. LIII; Theodoret, Haer.; and Frabricius II:6).

TRACT BAVA BATHRA: On Psalm 110, Melchizedek as its author.

TREGELLES: See translation of Heb. 7:1-13 in New Testament, 1852-1872.

TWENTIETH CENTURY NEW TESTAMENT: See Heb. 7.

WESCOTT: See his "Epistle to the Hebrews" in Greek with English Commentary, p. 171.

WILSON: See his "Emphatic Diaglott" of Heb. 7.

WYCLIFFE: N. T., version of 1380 (See Purvey's Revision of 1388, on Heb 7.

BERESHITH-RABBA: Section 43, folio 42, "The justifier of those who dwell in him."

BERRY: Interlinear Greek-English New Testament on Heb. 7:1-13.

BOOK OF THE COMBAT OF ADAM: See Canaan therein as father of Melchizedek.

CATENA ARABICA: See on Genesis 1. Melchizedek as son of Heraclis the son of Peleg.

CHRONICON PASCHALE: See page 49, 1688 edition of C. du Fresne du Cange, Paris.

CATHOLIC MASSES: See X Cath. Ency. pp. 8, 157, and Vol. III, p. 264.

CLEMENT OF ALEXANDRIA: Bk. II, Misc., Ch. 5.

COMMENTARIES ON MELCHIZEDEK IN THE OLD TESTAMENT:
Baumgarten: Old Testament Commentary on Psalm 110, p. 182.
Bahr: "Symbolik I:179

Delitzsch: See Lange, Crit. Doc & Hom. Comm. on Ps. 110, p. 406

Lange: Crit. Doc. & Hom. Comm. on Ps. 110, p. 406.

Murphy: Commentary on Ps. 110, p. 289.

Mant: 1822 Ed. of Common Prayer Book of Church of England, on Ps. 110.

Clarke: See Commentary on Genesis 14:18 on the meaning of "Malki-tsedek."

Smith: William Robertson, with S. A. Cook: Ency. Brit. Vo. 18 (11th Ed.) p. 92.

CYPRIAN: Chapter 4, Epistle to Caecilius No. 62.

DE ROSSI and KENNICOTT: SEE CLARKE, supra. Collection of manuscripts on "al dibrathi."

DOUAY VERSION OF 1582: See Heb. 7:1-13.

EISENMENGER: "Neuentdektes Judenthum (Konigsburg, 1711) on Midrash traditions.

EPIPHANIUS: Haer. 55:2, on parentage of Melchizedek.

FABRICIUS: Codex Pseud. Part V. Vol. 1, p. 311, on Enoch, Elias and Melchizedek.

GEORGIUS CEDRENUS: (Goar's Ed.) Vol. 1, p. 27, Melchizedek as son of Sidos.

GESENIUS: Robinson's English-Hebrew Edition of 1844, p. 892 on "malki-tsedek."

GOLDEN BOUGH, Frazer.: Vol. 5, p. 17, on Canaanitish origin of Melchizedek.

HASTINGS: "Melchizedek" in his Dictionary of Christ and the Gospels, on Heb. 7.

HIPPOLYTUS: Refutation of All Heresies, Book 7, Ch. 24, and Book 10, Ch. 20.

IGNATIUS: Ch. IV, Epistle to the Philadelphians, on priesthoods.

INSTITUTES OF LACTANTIUS: Book IV. Ch. 14, p. 214 (Edinburgh Ed. Ante-Nicene Fathers).

JEROME: 73rd Epistle, identifying Melchizedek with the Holy Ghost.

JOSEPHUS BEN GORIOM: Book 6, Chapter 35 on identity of Jehoram and Melchizedek.

JOSEPHUS: Antiquities of the Jews, Book 1, Ch. 10, Sec. 2.

JUSTIN MARTYR: Dialogue with Trypho, Chapter 63, and also 118.

JAMES VERSION: AV of Heb. 7:1-13.